W9-BCU-015

CHURCH AND POLITICS

Enda McDonagh

CHURCH AND POLITICS

From Theology to a
Case History of Zimbabwe

University of Notre Dame Press
Notre Dame, Indiana

196400

University of Notre Dame Press edition 1980
Published in Ireland as *The Demands of Simple Justice*
This edition published by arrangement with
Gill and Macmillan, Dublin
Printed in the United States of America

Library of Congress Cataloging in Publication Data

McDonagh, Enda.
   Church and politics.

   Bibliography: p.
   1. Christianity and politics. 2. Catholic
Church in Zimbabwe—History. 3. Church and state
in Zimbabwe—History. 4. Zimbabwe—Church history.
I. Title.
BR115.P7M314   261.7   80-53070
ISBN 0-268-00734-9

The real issues must be faced; discrimination based on race must be eliminated, equality of opportunity must be guaranteed; there must be proper parliamentary representation, job reservation must go, land reform must be seriously tackled with more equitable distribution and appropriate control. These are reasonable demands. They are the reasonable demands of simple justice . . .

Reconciliation in Rhodesia, Rhodesian Catholic Bishops' Conference, January 1974

Contents

Introduction

In April/May 1977 a meeting of a representative group of the Catholic church in Rhodesia (as it then was) took place at Driefontein to discuss the current and future challenges facing the church. The discussions took place in the shadow of an escalating war which affected very closely the lives of the majority of Catholic clergy, religious and laity scattered throughout Rhodesia. One of the most deeply felt and strongly expressed needs of the people present was for some theological analysis of and pastoral guidance on the violence which was becoming all-embracing. Some earlier attempts by the local church to arrive at some agreed analysis and guidance had never reached maturity. It was suggested that a European theologian with some knowledge of the matter be approached. In January 1978 I was invited to undertake such a study. Unfortunately, I was not free at the time but after some discussion on the scope and limitations of the task involved, I agreed to attempt it at a later date. With due allowance for the differences in scope and responsibility which were agreed, this book resulted from my accepting the invitation to begin such a study in April 1978.

The differences in scope from those of the original suggestion at Driefontein are at least hinted at in the sub-title. The reasons for change may be briefly explained. It did not seem to me useful or even possible to attempt theological and moral analysis or assessment of the war and violence in Rhodesia without placing it in its political context. War and violence as instruments of political defence or change can only be understood and evaluated by giving due attention to

1

the political context. I feel very much confirmed in this view as a result of my study.

In the Rhodesian and other contemporary situations, it would not be adequate to seek guidance for individual Christians and treat the community of Christians, the church, as somehow above and outside politics and history. The Christian is a communal being. The Catholic church in particular is very conscious of its corporate, historical existence. The Catholic church in Rhodesia had, even more than other churches, become a focus at least of controversy, among its own adherents and the politically engaged, for its stand on various issues directly affecting politics and the war. So a theological analysis of the relationship between church and politics, including the political problems of war and violence, seemed the appropriate route to take.

At this stage a new difficulty presented itself. While I had been to Rhodesia in the summer of 1973 and had kept in touch in a general way, I was not an expert in the complex political, economic, social, racial and religious conditions, past and present, of that country nor could I have become one in the time available. I could not in other words hope to write a report or book simply and exclusively about Rhodesia. It was arranged that I should visit Rhodesia again on a couple of occasions, which I did. The cooperation of the many people involved and the exposure to various viewpoints and circumstances were a tremendous help. I received further help in discussion with people of varied experience and expertise in Europe, particularly in Britain, Ireland, and Switzerland as well as in my own reading. But I still did not feel that I could present a full and convincing analysis of church and politics in Rhodesia.

I was strengthened in this feeling by the awareness that theological analyses of church and politics were undergoing serious shifts in the Catholic church itself. Although movement had begun well before Vatican II, the documents of the latter on religious liberty and on the Church in the Modern World intensified and expanded that movement. The emergence of Christian-Marxist dialogue, of political and liberation theologies and a deepening sense of the church's mission of social justice had all changed the discussion on the traditional church-state structure as it was conducted even in the liberating and sophisticated terms employed by Jacques Maritain and John Courtney Murray. To respond to Rhodesian needs it would first of all be necessary to explore and systematise some current thinking in church and politics.

Such exploration and systematisation should, however, be undertaken in the light of Rhodesian history and experience. So my visit to Rhodesia to acquire as much first-hand knowledge of the situation as possible had also a theological significance and I prepared a preliminary report on that visit, indicating my understanding of the situation and an outline of the proposed theological and moral study. After a second visit in autumn 1978, during which I discussed the report and the situation with individuals and groups, I settled down to plan and prepare this book.

As I made clear in the 1978 report, I was trying to formulate a theological understanding of the relation between church and politics in the light of the problems and insights offered by the Rhodesian and other contemporary situations and in turn use this developing theological understanding to illuminate the Rhodesian situation. The circularity involved need not be vicious and may be inevitable. Rhodesian experience certainly shaped my further formulation of the questions but I brought to that experience my own earlier experience of other situations, the questions and the provisional answers of an earlier phase of understanding. The resources I brought to Rhodesia were challenged and extended in the search for a more accurate formulation of the questions. In a two-stage response a new systematic understanding emerged for me which had then to be more precisely and fully elaborated in the Rhodesian situation. Such a concrete elaboration is limited by the competence of the writer and the complexity of the situation. It is also contingent and provisional because of the very movement of history. Yet it is a necessary stage in enabling the church to orientate itself in this very movement of history. Such an orientation, provided it is based on adequate information and analysis, will have the strength and sense of direction to enable church leaders to develop missionary goals, policies and strategies for a reasonable period. The provisional character of the analysis persists in the face of the continuing historical movement and change. The experience of doing the analysis and trying to implement it will provide guidelines and confidence in this inevitable revision and renewal.

The complex movements or dialectics between thecry and practice, between analysis, policy making and implementation, between the resources, structures and needs of changing historical situations, sometimes issue in rigid adherence to a particular policy formed in quite different historical circumstances and no longer appropriate, or in confusion of thought and accompanying paralysis of action. This work with its mediating structure from exposure-to-situation to reflection-on-theological-tradition   to   analysis-of-situation-in-light-of-theology is intended to overcome the threats of rigidity and parlaysis and at the same time provide a stimulus and some model of how a more adequate theology and practice may be sought in the future. It is obviously not the last word as there can never be a historical last word. But to be worthwhile at all it should provide the first word in a new phase of analysing and living the relations between church and politics in Rhodesia.

I leave further development of this argument to a later presentation of the method and structure of the finished work and finally to its practical realisation.

Responsibility

I mentioned earlier a certain change in the responsibility for performing the task, completing the study and finally publishing it. The initiative came from the Catholic church in Zimbabwe/Rhodesia. The church or at least many of its members were anxious for a study of the violence and then of the church's relations to politics and political change including the use of violence. The facilities and cooperation which the church provided for this author were a clear endorsement of that original initiative and invitation. The project was financed through the Bethlehem Fathers, a very prestigious missionary group of Swiss origin. Continuous consultation and monitoring of various drafts by members of the Rhodesian church had significant influence in shaping the work at all its formative stages. In a very important sense this book belongs to the Catholic church in Rhodesia and its primary purpose is to serve that church. Yet it was clear at a very early stage that this was to be my work. I was taking responsibility for it. Only I would have the final say in what went into it. Only I would be accountable for what it said, good or bad, true or false. It would also be my responsibility to have it published. Its contents or publication would in no way commit the church in Rhodesia. I hope that it will serve the Rhodesian church and not contain material damaging or offensive to that church because of its falsity or ineptitude. But the material, writing and publication is my sole responsibility. Whatever use the church may make of it will be its business but it has no prior responsibility for what appears here.

This may appear to be labouring a rather obvious point. The Rhodesian church has suffered too much in recent decades both for what it did and did not do, from opponents and critics in government, against government, within its own adherents and outside them to justify taking any risks of misunderstanding now. My gratitude to, concern and respect for the various members of the church of very differing ecclesiological and political viewpoints, demands that I make it absolutely clear who is responsible for the historical account, theological understanding and moral evaluation printed here. It was on this basis that I was given and accepted the generous advice and cooperation of so many people who would not agree with all or perhaps any of my analysis and conclusions.

The Rhodesian Connections

Having undertaken the project, I visited Rhodesia in April/May 1978. My first (unpublished) report contains an account of that visit, published here as an appendix. At this point I wish to record briefly how that and a subsequent visit in September/October affected the genesis and structure of this work.

The organisation of the visits was the work of the Catholic

church through the Bethlehem Fathers, the Commission for
Justice and Peace, Salisbury, and the Catholic Institute for
International Relations, London. It proved very effective for
me. With the cooperation of the Catholic bishops I visited
each diocese and prefecture and had very thorough and frank
conversations with bishops, clergy, and laity. These conversations on my earlier visit helped me to formulate the critical
questions affecting the church and proved very influential
in the final shape of this work. My return visit in September/
October was devoted to discussion of my earlier report and
challenged me to deeper and more critical examination and
reflection.

Direct contact with the Rhodesian church continued as I
prepared drafts of chapters of the final report. Again through
the good offices of the Catholic Institute for International
Relations I had meetings in December 1978, January 1979 and
June 1979 with various specialists in theology and in Rhodesian
church affairs, as well as with newly-returned missionaries to
discuss the draft chapters. Other members of the Rhodesian
church and the theological community provided written criticism and assistance and have continued this assistance.

All this gave a sense of immediacy to the Rhodesian
situation and of involvement with it, enabling me to share
something of the 'insider' feel I believe to be important in
understanding such situations. It has kept alive over the period
of writing this work (longer than I anticipated or like) the
dialectic and the tension between reflection and experience,
between political theory and practice, between social analysis
and personal understanding, between academic theology and
pastoral concern, between the universal church context and
that of the local church in Rhodesia. The structure of this
work as a whole and of the particular sections derives from
and depends on these dialectical relationships and tensions.
How far I have been able to discern, understand, analyse and
communicate them only the reader can assess. Without the
assistance of so many members of the Rhodesian church I
could not have even made the attempt.

The Structure and the Method

The basic structure of this work is very simple. In the first major section I examine, develop and try to synthesise a contemporary theology of church and politics. In the second major section I examine relevant aspects of the Rhodesian situation in the light of that theology. Of course, as I have already emphasised, the theology was not taken from the wind or even from a reading of books, current and classical. Theological literature old and new played its role but my reading and thinking was shaped by the experience and needs of the church of Rhodesia and in the world at large as I know them. In seeking to establish this dialogue between church and politics, I tried to take account of tradition as fully as possible, the normative tradition of Scripture and the historical tradition of subsequent church involvement and theology. Without such fidelity to tradition one could not maintain the genuine continuity and identity of church or theology. Yet fidelity to tradition involves openness to change, sometimes radical change as tradition demonstrates in the rejection of the judaising practice (a classical church-politics problem) or the acceptance of the Constantinian (Theodosian) establishment or, to come to contemporary events, the final breach with that establishment delineated in the major documents of Vatican II on the church, religious freedom and the Church in the Modern World.

The cul-de-sac out of which Vatican II and some of its theological advisors like John Courtney Murray finally took the church, was a nostalgic relic of the 'Constantinian' structure, established by the state, of one true church in society, and tolerance, at best, for the professors and practitioners of other churches and faiths or of none. Some of the nostalgia and the relics are still around and in churches other than the Catholic. However, Vatican II initiated or at least made initial advances in a new emancipation of the Catholic church, for the Constantinian emancipation had become an enslavement in structures (witness the concordats with Hitler's Germany) and in mentality (witness the silencing of Father Murray in the later fifties and early sixties). It is sometimes easier to

shed the trappings of slavery than to find useful alternatives.
The search for alternatives still goes on. In the time available
and in face of the variety of problems facing church and
society in first, second and third worlds, it would be impossible to expect such alternatives as are proposed to be fully
developed, widely applicable and universally agreed. It is
doubtful if there will ever be a doctrine on church and politics
aspiring to the universality and uniformity of the kind
demanded by the recent manuals of Public Ecclesiastical Law.
The political plurality of the world today excludes such a
prospect.

Yet the very continuity and universality of the church,
for all its rich local diversity and challenges, calls for some
continuity in understanding if not in strategy, in theology if
not in pastoral practice throughout the world. The gradual
compression of the world into a global village reinforces that
need. But to discover, maintain and permanently revise such
continuity in understanding while being fully sensitive to the
diversity of local demand is a daunting task. To some extent
it is the task of this book, the method and structure of which
indicates one way of approaching this task. Aware of the
tradition in thought and life, the theologian seeks to immerse
himself in a particular local church facing critical political
challenges. Emerging from that situation he tries, through
dialogue with classical and contemporary theological commentary on such situations, to provide a fresh theological
structure with which he turns once more to the Rhodesian
situation. Of course the theological structure is inadequate
and the application to the Rhodesian situation still more so.
But it may be that this struggle to move between the two and
root his thinking in the theological tradition will provide
some immediate guidance for church people urgently engaged
with Zimbabwe/Rhodesia, and at least a stimulus to do better
for theologians who confront similar challenges.

The details of the structure are indicated in the table of
contents and will be rather laboriously spelled out in the
contents themselves. It may be useful however to reflect
briefly on two theological aspects of the method and goal
of this book which do not figure in the systematic treatment
which follows.

The first of these concerns the propriety and value of attempting to mediate theologically between the concrete complex problems of a particular historical situation such as Rhodesia and the more abstract and inevitably simplifying doctrinal tradition of the church. The difficulties are enormous as this book will amply demonstrate. It is one thing to develop a theology of the Christian's commitment to justice or the church's obligation to promote the values of the kingdom in society; it is quite another to express this in terms of what Christian and church action should be in regard to gross inequality in income or discrimination in education. To consider the theological merits of the 'just war theory' as against those of 'non-violence' makes a fascinating debate for theologians. It becomes a matter of life and death for the politically and pastorally engaged in a situation like Rhodesia. And the translation of the debate and its results, however vigorously pursued, are both difficult and risky in the actual war situation. Should theologians pursue their 'games' in academe? Should pastors and faithful despair of any relevant guidance from them? If we are to have a thoughtful and caring Christian church and an authentic incarnate faith, the answers are clearly no. But the responsiblities of both sides are enormous to share in a collaborative effort which engages the most knowledgeable, the most thoughtful, the most committed and the most active members of the church in pursuit of the single goal of understanding and doing the truth of Jesus Christ in actual historical situations.

The intellectual tasks of the theologians are critical but they must be fulfilled in dialogue with the pastors. Without pastoral dialogue and engagement, theology lacks the bite of living faith. Of course political situations and problems are not the only area of pastoral responsibility. Indeed it is only recently they have taken a prominent role. And it would be a pity if politics in the usual narrow sense became, by virtue of the pendulum principle, the dominant pastoral concern of theologians or pastors. The dictum that 'everything is politics' is too easily misleading for theologians and politicians as the necessary distinction between society and state, developed later in the book, clearly shows. Making faith and church a purely private matter is no longer acceptable but neither is it acceptable to see everything in terms of politics.

My point here however is not to rehearse the debate but to insist on the need for pastoral engagement by theologians and theological engagement by pastors. This does not mean a confusion of function or the abandonment of necessary specialisation but effective cooperation and real dialogue. The praxis of pastors is critical to theological reflection, the questions and conclusions of theologians are essential to the health of the church; for their own health they need to be closely connected with the busy, struggling people of God which is the church.

The second aspect of the theological investigation I wish to discuss here is one which might easily be overlooked and even rejected as quite inappropriate to theology as such. The ultimate goal of the writer and, I would hope, the readers of this book is some increased understanding of how the kingship, ruling, empowering and loving presence of God is to be discerned and responded to in historical situations such as that of Zimbabwe/Rhodesia. The method and criteria of discernment and response form the substance of the book. Yet they do not constitute a self-contained structure. Apart from their contingent and provisional character, leaving them in constant need of revision, they have validity only in so far as they open readers and writer up to the divine presence. Theology is always some reflection and instrument of the search for God. A theologian is a seeker after God, not just a scientific commentator on other people's searches, past, present or future. In writing this book I hope to share in some small portion in the opening to God which contemporary political situations embody, however ambiguously, and more particularly in the opening to God which the Rhodesian situation embodies. I hope to share in the faith of the Rhodesian church and share with it some of the possibilities for growth in incarnate faith which theological analysis offers. Such 'pious aspirations' may not inhibit the rigour and the risk of theological activity. The rigour is all the more necessary if the attendant risks of misleading a church and finally distorting God are to be avoided. But this scientific rigour forms part of the ascesis of theologians and church as they seek a purified, more authentic awareness of God present in history and society.

Acknowledgements

My general debt to the Rhodesian church, its bishops, clergy and laity has already been to some extent acknowledged. It would be hard for me to exaggerate the generosity and understanding which I encountered on my visits there and in my meetings with Rhodesian church members elsewhere. The critical help was matched by the warm hospitality, of which I may take the Irish Carmelite Fathers in Salisbury to be particularly representative as they had to suffer me more than anybody else. The particular individuals who helped are so numerous that I could not realistically publish a full list. Perhaps I may mention Archbishop Patrick Chakaipa as symbolic of all the bishops, Father Randolph SJ as representative of all the Church officials, Father Amstutz SMB as representing his own society and other missionary groups and individuals, John Deary as representing the laity and the Commission for Justice and Peace, Ismael Muvingi as representing my African friends and Tim Sheehy as one of the many involved in the enormous work done by the Catholic Institute of International Relations.

November 1979

PART I

Faith and Politics in the Making of Theology

1.

Christian Faith and Social Justice

Introduction

Contemporary Christian preoccupation with justice in society
is evident in every country in which the Christian churches
work and at every level of these churches themselves. From
Salisbury to Santiago bishops, theologians and plain believers
find themselves wrestling with the teaching and practice of
justice. While the practice must always pose its problems it
might be thought that in the wake of almost ninety years of
papal, conciliar, episcopal and theological pronouncements,
the teaching would be clear, systematic, comprehensive and
agreed. In its general formulations and exhortations the
teaching is clear and agreed. Systematic theological analysis
of the basic relationship between Christian faith and social
justice is not so readily available. And its practical implications involving pastoral priorities and commitments do not
always enjoy clarity or command agreement. It will be the
task of this chapter to attempt such a systematic theological
analysis in the hope of providing a basis for both clarity and
agreement at the practical and pastoral levels.

Sources, Method, Goal

Even a survey of all the relevant written material on this topic
from Old and New Testaments through Christian tradition to
more recent official documents and current theology would
far exceed the limits of this study. These sources will be
taken largely for granted and for the most part only implicitly
invoked in the more systematic presentation attempted here.

On this issue these documents biblical, doctrinal and theological reflect in their different ways the continuing human struggle to interpret and express faith in God as determining just relations between men. The primary and normative expression in the Bible provides the starting point and prevailing standard. It can only be understood in the context of the community tradition of the church itself and of the dialogue between word and world in which that tradition emerged and develops. God's Word is always enfleshed in a historical world becoming thereby accessible to the men of that world but running the risk of dying with that world or at least of becoming obscure and distorted for men of a different world. The ecclesial and theological tasks of understanding and appropriating anew the living Word of God for a new world and a new generation create fresh challenges for the church and the maintainers and developers of its tradition. As primarily concerned with the Catholic church, I take that as my starting point.

In the area of faith and justice, Leo XIII, Pius XI, Pius XII, John XXIII and Paul VI have proved themselves outstanding maintainers and developers of tradition. Their encyclical letters, particularly *Rerum Novarum* (1891), *Quadragesimo Anno* (1931), *Mater et Magistra* (1961), *Pacem in Terris* (1963), *Populorum Progressio* (1966) and *Octagesima Adveniens* (1971), express a developing understanding of a changing world and its demands in a living word which is both exciting and awesome in its achievement. Further documents such as those of Pius XII on Human Rights (1941), of Vatican II on the Church in the Modern World (1965), of the Synod of Bishops on Justice in the World (1971) and Evangelisation (1974), of the Latin American Episcopal Conference at Medellin (1968), of the Irish Bishops' Conference (1977), the Canadian Bishops' Conference (1976) and the meetings of the Rhodesian Catholic Bishops' Conference through the sixties and seventies, reinforce the impression of the Catholic church as providing leadership not only for its own adherents but for all mankind in the discernment and promotion of a just society throughout the world.

In this the Catholic church has not been alone. Apart from

secular organisations and their achievements such as the UN Declaration on Human Rights and other covenants and conventions, the other Christian churches individually and through the World Council of Churches have displayed similar growth in understanding and commitment. As an obvious field for shared understanding and activity the search for social justice has released a great deal of ecumenical energy and deepened the bonds uniting the churches. Formal endorsement and encouragement of this has developed at the highest level through the institution of Sodepax, relating and coordinating the work, with central offices at Rome and Geneva.[1]

At the theological level the churches have been no less productive and no less ecumenical but perhaps inevitably somewhat more diverse and divergent. The diversity and divergency reflect much less denominational difference than regional, cultural, ethnic and 'class' difference. Political, liberation and developmental or even revolutionary theologies flourish in the same church as more conventional or classical theological approaches to the problem of justice in society. To present and evaluate the whole range would be considerably more difficult and space-consuming than surveying the official documents and would render the study unduly long and complex. Some of the more valuable and established insights of these rich if still conflicting theological developments will, it is hoped, be integrated together with the achievements of the papal and episcopal statements in this attempt to provide a systematic exploration and presentation of the relationship between Christian faith and social justice.

This study was prompted by the interests and needs of the Roman Catholic church in Rhodesia. Because of that and because of the background of the author it will be primarily a Roman Catholic study in its sources, methods and goals. As I have already indicated, there is considerable convergence in thinking between the main-line Christian churches, their documents and theologians, on the issues to be raised here. In Zimbabwe as elsewhere this must be a source of strength and clarity in any particular church's understanding and witness.

More critical to the goal and to the method of the enterprise is the Rhodesian reference point. The theologian as systematic analyst and expositor may easily lose his contact with the realities of injustice and the struggle for justice in an actual situation. Yet he can never master the actuality of a complex and constantly changing social process. He can at best hope to experience and appropriate (too crudely) some of the mood, movement and more significant features which dominate a situation for some observable time. In this way he may be able to speak out of it with some insider feel and perception. Because this situation is part of a wider and longer historical process to which he also belongs, there is an important sense in which every theologian speaks *to* the situation, from outside as it were. It is some combination of insider involvement and outsider perspective that makes for the best theological analysis. The insider-outsider proportions vary from author to author and work to work. In this study this author, for the reasons already noted in the Introduction, enjoys much more of the outsider perspective and finds himself trying to speak more decisively to the situation. The insider balance will need to be partially supplied by others, particularly by the many involved, perceptive and analytical fellow-Christians who attempted to educate him in Rhodesia.

The work may enjoy the strengths of its limitations: distance and perspective that illuminate while not being detached from the complex, painful, even tragic, reality. At any rate the author must try to maintain the interaction between the wider social and historical context and the more immediate Rhodesian situation, between his outsider and insider stances. This could and should be reflected in a number of different approaches. In this work, as the Introduction suggested, I will try to express my insider-outsider understanding in more general systematic terms in the opening chapters. They have been decisively influenced by my Rhodesian experience but envisage a wider audience. It is from experiences such as Rhodesia that the church at large learns and develops its theological understanding. In the closing chapters the focus will be more directly on Rhodesia and on how this developed Christian understanding is or should be enfleshed there.

The overall method of the work then is based on distinctions and interactions and mutual inferences that amount to a series of dialectics between word and world, faith and action, the understanding and witness of the Catholic church and that of other Christian churches, the past and the present, the achieved and the yet to be, leading to the systematic dialectic between Christian theology and an analysis of social justice set in the interaction between the generic world situation and the more specific Rhodesian context.

Social Morality for Christians

The justice we are concerned with here is justice in society, a moral quality of human relationships and structures as they cohere to form a particular or worldwide society. While it is possible to delimit the range of structures and relationships and to identify a limited society such as that of Rhodesia, it is not possible to isolate that society from the wider set of relationships and structures, political, cultural and religious, by which it interacts with the wider African and global society. The difficulties of isolation in a sphere as confined as the economic have already been brutally exposed in the 'sanctions-busting' story.

As a moral quality social justice is intimately related to Christian faith. The ethical monotheism of the Old Testament was irrevocably ethical. Faith in Yahweh commanded and demanded a moral behaviour in relation to mankind that was basic to good human society and reflected God's own relationship to man. The righteousness of God which some commentators see as the dominant theme of the Old Testament[2] and even of the New, provides the criterion for human response, judgment upon failures in it and the source of forgiveness and power in overcoming these failures. The more explicitly ethical teaching of the Decalogue (law) and the prophets embodies for human relationships the more precise demands for Israel and mankind which derive from the covenanted gift of divine righteousness. In the New Testament or covenant, the gift takes the form of Jesus Christ, only-begotten of the Father; the righteousness is presented in all its divine depths of gift and call, judgment and saving power.

Its range is all mankind, its basis divine sonship, its model the love, life and death of Jesus Christ, its guarantee his resurrection and the gift of the Spirit, its ultimate criterion whatever one does to 'these least ones', the hungry, the sick, the prisoners, the oppressed.

In the renewal of moral analysis within the Catholic tradition which has taken place over the last twenty-five years, the biblical basis and the centrality of Jesus Christ have resumed their proper roles. Morality for Catholics and other Christians is now presented in terms of discipleship of Jesus Christ rather than, as in the manuals, as obedience to laws. The social dimensions of discipleship have not been thoroughly worked through as yet. However, that the discipleship ethic is a community or social ethic scarcely needs much elaboration. In the original call to discipleship given to Abraham, as well as in the covenant established with the people of Israel through Moses, the emphasis was on God's election of and call to a people, a community. As the call was given to a community to behave in a certain way, so understanding of that call is possible only in a community. The composition of the bible itself bears witness to that. It is a community book in its very creation and acceptance. And the formidable moral criticisms and challenges of the prophets were directed in the name of their God to a people. The goal of the gift, call and behaviour was the formation of the community of God's people and the emergence of the social reality of his kingdom. It was this social reality which Jesus preached, for which he died, and which he inaugurated by his life, death and resurrection and embodied in symbol and reality in the new Israel of the church. Given to a community, possible of understanding only in a community and directed towards the formation of a community, the Judaeo-Christian ethic is indisputably a social ethic. The moral demands of discipleship or its way of life are inseparably social.

The social character of discipleship morality might be elaborated in terms of invitation and following of Christ (*Nachfolge Christi*), in terms of the two great commandments of love and their unbreakable unity, in terms of the preaching, promotion and establishment of the inbreaking kingdom of God. Such elaborations provide a stimulus, a moral direction, a theological basis and ultimate perspective for the social commitment and engagement which are essential to Christian understanding and living. A more precise and critical analysis of the relationship between Christian faith and social morality will incorporate such insights while attending more fully to the distinction and interaction between faith and morality and to the structures and values of social morality which may need to be unpacked from the hold-all of social justice.

Distinction and Interaction of Faith and Social Morality/Justice

The discipleship approach to Christian morality restored, as I have said, morality to its biblical base and Christological centre. The distinction and interaction of faith and morality derive from this base and centre although that may be sometimes obscured in some over-simple or undifferentiated presentations. From the historical Decalogue to the prophetic to the wisdom literature, the writings of the Old Testament indicate that faith in Yahweh demands moral behaviour and that moral failure contradicts and eventually undermines faith. Yet the moral teaching itself is shared with a wider world and the sinner (in his moral failure) may go on believing, indeed must go on believing if he is to be rescued from his failures. The synoptic gospels with the two great commandments, as well as the Sermon on the Mount and the parables of the kingdom, illuminate the moral life of faith but with due attention to the distinction and interaction between morality and faith. So do the Pauline lists of gifts of the Spirit, failures which exclude from the kingdom and moral exhortations in personal, domestic and social life. The letter of James expresses the same distinction and interaction very clearly and forcibly.

Insistence on this distinction and interaction between faith and morality is not a matter of intellectual sensitivity or academic purity. No church is an island. Social structures and relationships calling for analysis and reform involve other

Christians, non-Christians and post-Christians. The analysis and reform cannot be completed without their understanding and good will. The distinction which Christians uphold allows for that common search, with men of every religious belief and none, for social moral values and their realisation. The interaction which they equally defend provides a judgment upon and stimulus to their own efforts and a sense of perspective and ultimate basis of judgment for all efforts. Discipleship translated into the promotion of social morality and justice may be understood, admired and assisted by people still blind to the source and centre of that discipleship, Jesus Christ. Social ethics can and should play a mediating role between believers and unbelievers and between Christian faith and the practical pursuit of a just society.

Incarnation, Natural Law and Social Justice

The distinctive, mediating role of social ethics for Christians turns on the doctrine of Incarnation. Jesus the man as incarnate God confirms the created value of the human person as formed from the dust of the earth in the image of God, overcomes the distortion of that image and renders the human and created transparent of and mediating of the creator and divine by participation in divine sonship. In the light of the incarnation, a person is called to become, in community, in history and in the cosmos, the expression of the transcendent, without thereby losing his humanity, indeed having it thereby renewed in its authenticity and fullness. The authentically and fully human is demanded and assured in Jesus Christ. Faith in Jesus Christ involves faith in the Father, the God of Abraham and of Moses, of the people of Israel and of all mankind. Discipleship of Jesus Christ, living out that faith, involves living an authentically and fully human life.[3] Thus truly human activity and life constitutes the moral task of discipleship, the morality of Christians. Discipleship, so far from distorting or short-circuiting the human, endorses and enlarges it. The moral values which derive from and promote true humanity are moral values of discipleship. In Catholic tradition these values have been globally designated by the term 'Natural Law'. This term has its own difficulty, as the model of nature invoked may have been in some respects misleading. It too easily reverted to 'biologism' and even where the personal as against the biological properly asserted itself, there was often insufficient attention to the social and historical character of human nature. In comparison with other Christian traditions the relations of sin and grace and nature were not clearly and adequately analysed.

Yet, the tradition had much that was basically sound. It kept alive the created basis of morality in the human condition and its openness to transcendence through the Incarnation. It provided a framework for critical and systematic understanding of the relation between faith and morality, and a basis for communication and cooperation with all men of good will in discerning and building a just society. The papal encyclicals, conciliar and episcopal statements on social ethics are expressed for the most part in the language and categories of this natural law tradition. In recent years they have tended to supplement that tradition with more directly biblical expressions and categories but with the overall effect of restoring the same tradition to its incarnational context and so renewing it, rather than replacing it. The statements by the Rhodesian Catholic Bishops' Conference reflect some of this development. At the same time the Reformed churches through their use of the terms and categories of 'the responsible society', for example, have begun to supplement and integrate their more directly biblical tradition with the insights of the natural law tradition. The convergence of the church traditions at this level of analysis is paralleled by their increasing practical cooperation in pursuit of justice in society.[4]

The discernment and promotion of the authentically and fully human constitutes the moral task for Christians and mankind. Such authentic humanity may be achieved only in and through society or community. Person-in-community and community-of-persons provide complementary and interacting sources or subjects and goals or objects of moral activity. The analysis of how person and community are to discern and promote the authentically human through the relationships and structures of a society defines social ethics.

In the broadest sense of the term and relating it to its biblical origins in divine righteousness, justice in society may be understood to apply to all these relationships and structures. The moral value of such relationships and structures depends on virtues traditionally and properly distinct, if not separable, from justice, virtues such as charity and truth. There is a close affinity between truthfulness in relationship and justice, and for the Christian a justice that is not an expression of the more profound relationship of charity is not fully justice. However, it is wiser not to attempt to discuss the whole of social morality under the rubric of justice. Taking the rather elementary traditional notion of justice as giving every man his 'due', one should explore the meaning of 'due' in the complex set of institutions, interactions and activities which constitute human life in society today.

The Social Meaning of 'Due'

In commutative or exchange justice the 'due' or *debitum* which had to be rendered to the other involved simply two contracting parties such as buyer and seller and was readily understood if not always so readily rendered. In social justice one is talking about much more complex dues arising through the structures of society between individuals and groups and not so readily discerned and understood. What can be said to be due to a group such as the unemployed, the handicapped, the racially different? On what basis? From whom is it due? How is the due identified and rendered?

The basis for 'due' in society returns to the dignity of the human person in secular terms and the source of that dignity in Christian terms, in the doctrine of incarnation, which also embraces creation, redemption and eschatology. Whatever is due to a person or group of persons rests on that inalienable dignity and its divine origins, significance and destiny.

The basis for 'due', human and Christian, indicates certain characteristics whose recognition should constitute the payment of that due. The first of these may be described in general terms as 'inviolability'. The dignity of the human being distinguishes him as a particular world in himself who is not simply derived from and may not be reduced to the wider social structures which remain essential to his existence and development. Without some social contact between his father and mother he would not exist at all. Without a wider social context including the parental or its equivalent he would not survive and develop. Yet he constitutes a particular if dependent and developing world of his own which may not be invaded, manipulated, eliminated or treated as simply an instance of humanity or unit of society. In this lies his inalienable dignity[5] while from this derives the inviolability of the human being which enters into a range of such 'dues' as respect for life and bodily integrity including immunity from torture and 'inhuman and degrading treatment', freedom of religion, association and expression.

That inviolability should be related to particular freedoms is intelligible when one remembers the positive qualities to which inviolability relates and its social context. Human inviolability refers to the unique and individual world which the human being with his capacity for personal knowledge, decision-making, creativity and relationship embodies at least potentially. That world is his free creation. In it he must enjoy freedom both psychological and social. His inviolability opens into his personal creativity with his potential to constitute a unique world of his own and so enrich the world about him and he should enjoy social immunity or freedom from invasion into or trespass on that particular world. Inviolability and freedom cohere as social 'dues' to a person's human dignity and potential creativity.

The inviolability and freedom are due to one's human dignity as a person, not to one's particular stage of development, talents or achievement. In that basic sense they are due equally to all. All human beings are equal in basic human dignity and are due the social context and protection in which they can realise and protect it. Equality is a third element in social justice to which recognition of human dignity commits us as human beings and Christians. The criticism made of equality as a human due, on the basis of different stages of development, personal or communal, either provides rationalisation for immoral self-interest and discrimination or else ignores the basic issues at stake. Of course the translation of such equality into social and political structures, relationships and activities is a complicated historical task. At least if one remembers that it is equality which must be translated and realised, one may avoid or strive to overcome the more obvious inequalities, discriminations and oppressions which, on the basis of race, sex and class, dominate so much of contemporary society. Equality must, like inviolability and freedom, be further spelled out so that one can relate it to the concepts of fairness in availability of goods, services and participation in decision-making. At this stage one is moving back to the interrelation with inviolability and freedom and moving forward to a detailed structure of social and political justice that ranges from fair trial to educational and employment oportunities to effective voice in government. All of this, whether expressed in human rights of the civil and political kind, so developed in the Western tradition, or the social and economic variety, more acceptable and urgent elsewhere, or in a more comprehensive exposition of justice in society, challenges the authenticity of contemporary discipleship. Acceptance of Jesus and the Incarnation cannot escape the demand to recognise and respond effectively to human beings in society in ways that respect their inviolability, freedom and equality. To reject any of these, in theory or practice, is to reject 'the least ones' whom Christ (*Matt.* 25) identified with himself. It is, for Christians, to contradict the faith they profess.

Social Justice, Pedagogue of Christian Faith

In exploring and justifying the Christian commitment to social justice, the primacy of faith in Jesus Christ and its 'performative' connection with justice to the neighbour provides the key. Christians, perhaps Christians above all, are obliged to respect the dignity of person-in-society by realising the values of inviolability, freedom, equality and participation. The relationship between faith and social justice is, however, not one-way. I have already indicated the dialectical interaction between faith and morality. It was an interaction well-known to the prophets — and the Old Testament in general — for whom social injustice as sin was a form of idolatry. Honouring God with one's lips while exploiting widow and orphan showed where one's heart and faith really were. Crying, 'Lord, Lord', while one neglected the neighbour did not in Jesus' terms qualify for entry into the kingdom by faith. On the other hand response to the needy neighbour counted, even for the totally ignorant, as response to Jesus, as faith in fact (*Matt.* 25).

Starting from this side of the dialectic not only allows for cooperation with the non-believer, it opens up the non-believer and believer to an awareness of the human, the mystery of the human. In doing so it may lead to some sensitivity to the ultimate mystery of which the human is the penultimate. Openness to the neighbour as demanded and realised in social justice does not necessarily or properly terminate at the neighbour but at his source and destiny in Yahweh, God of Jesus Christ, eternal Father. In this way the discernment and promotion of social justice provides a pedagogy of the faith, a learning and experience that has the capacity, under the attracting power of the self-giving and revealing God whom we are encountering in the neighbour, to be transcended into explicit recognition of God, into faith. Not only does faith demand social justice, social justice finally demands faith — for the believer, increases in faith.

Conclusion

For all the concern with faith and social ethics, the relationship emerges more as that of the individual in relation to his God and his neighbour, albeit in society. The source or subject of both faith and ethical relationship has been predominantly individual. A great deal of discussion in this area follows this pattern. The Christian as agent in social ethics is predominantly the individual and particularly the lay individual. The apostolate of the laity has to a certain extent hinged on the *civis idem et christianus*,[6] the lay citizen in industry and politics certainly. Yet Christian faith is irreducibly communal. The Christian is Christian only as member

of community. Ethics for Christians as Christians is inescap-
ably community ethics. It is as community, as church, that
Christians have to live out their discipleship, not as individuals. How does this affect one's approach to social justice and
political morality as subject rather than object, from the side
of the agent rather than that of the patient or social recipient
of moral response? Can and must the church be morally
active as church? Does the believing community have as community a role in social and political ethics? These questions
will be my concern in the following chapter as I try to relate
the believing community of disciples and the political community of citizens in their distinction and interaction in
discerning and promoting social justice.

2.

The Believing Community and the Political Community

Church, Kingdom, Society and State

The long and tangled tale of 'church-state' relations has no final and universally acceptable resolution in sight. Given the changing historical character of both 'institutions' no such final resolution is feasible. Yet critical changes in theory and practice are occurring throughout the first, second and third worlds. The advent of a bishop from the second world to the See of Peter, historically entrenched in the first world but increasingly preoccupied with the third world, underlines the complexity of discerning even a general structure of relationship which might serve to enable churchmen or states-men to avoid some of the destructive confrontations of the past. At the theoretical level the developing theology of the church in itself and in its relation to other churches, religions and the secular world, found significant expression in the documents of Vatican II as well as in the great social encyc-licals of Popes John and Paul. In the same period momentous changes took place in the relations between church authorities and civil authorities from eastern Europe to Southern Africa to Latin America. Old patterns are being broken but the diversity and uncertainty are such that the new patterns are obscure or underdeveloped. This chapter attempts to reflect on the theoretical and practical changes still in operation in the hope of releasing churchmen and statesmen from the in-hibiting influence of outmoded mental categories. It seeks a reconsideration of the basic realities involved in 'church-state' relations. It would be too much to expect, however, that any-thing more than a sketch or rough outline of basic structures will emerge. In so far as it accurately reveals those structures its detailed filling in may be left to the individual situation and its individual problems.

The Traditional Duality and its Contemporary Expression

Historically, the 'church-state' problem derived from the duality of allegiance, community and authority which the Christian faith introduced into political life and, in particular, into the Roman Empire. Duties to God and Caesar proved a source of difficulty even unto death, as long as Caesar made divine or absolute claims. With the emergence of Christians from the catacombs into the basilicas, the difficulty did not disappear because the duality, however ignored or obscured, could never finally be erased. The difficulty focused on the duality of the two authorities as symbolised by the two swords of Pope Gelasius and their more sophisticated derivatives down through the Middle Ages. The pre-Vatican II classical expression of this tradition in the 'two perfect societies', as presented by Leo XIII, endeavoured to enlarge the understanding of the duality beyond the scope of authority relations and take particular account of the rather different vision of state and its authority which the American and French revolutions and the rise of liberal democracy had produced. Pius XI and Pius XII extended some of these ideas especially in the light of their experience of Nazism, Fascism and Communism.

Despite the developments from Leo to Pius XII, the thrust of Catholic teaching and practice was towards a reduction of church and state to their respective authorities. Whether in the ideal Catholic state or in the unavoidably separated, mixed or secular, state, church authorities dealt with state authorities for some obvious practical reasons. More profoundly, however, Catholics had been accustomed to think of the church as acting or teaching only in terms of the hierarchy or the pope acting or teaching. Citizens with or without church allegiance still predominantly saw the state as over against themselves and in its actions as distinct from themselves. It too was identified primarily with the institutions of government and the people who commanded them. Concordats, establishment and even conflict centred about this model of one supreme authority relating to and sometimes confronting the other. The days of popes and emperors might no longer reach the high personal drama of a Canossa, but the duality readily reduced to popes or hierarchies and governments, prime ministers or dictators.

How far this is no longer an appropriate model for 'church-state' relations is the burden of this chapter. The fuller reasons in theology and political philosophy will be considered presently. One evident ecclesial objection to such reductionism presents itself immediately. While the princes of this world enjoy a certain kind of power and authority, that does not apply in the mind of Jesus to his disciples. Yet the relationship, as frequently conceived and more frequently realised throughout the history of the church, reduced to a struggle of authorities, a power-struggle, and sometimes in very crude personal terms. By being drawn into such a power-struggle, the church was at best distorting and at worst surrendering its real authority and mission. In such circumstances its victories could be as calamitous as its defeats, as even Canossa might confirm. In its current conception of itself as the pilgrim and servant people of God, such power struggles have little appeal. Yet the duality and its attendant potential for conflict will not simply disappear. Some reconsideration of how church and state relate is clearly imperative.

Religious Freedom and its Implications

The most critical contribution to a reconsideration of this topic to emerge from Vatican II was the Declaration on Religious Freedom. Other documents, mentioned earlier and dealing with the church and its role in today's world, have enormous importance for the discussion. Yet the Declaration more clearly departed from accepted Catholic positions in escaping the old 'error has no rights' trap, implicitly rejecting the 'Catholic state' thesis, basing religious freedom firmly on the dignity of the human person and recognising the state's incompetence in religious affairs. This last point confirms and refines the historic duality in a context and in a manner which will, I believe, prove immensely fruitful in attempts to rethink the duality and relationship.

Exclusion of state competence in religion undermines, as it was always intended to, any claims to absolutism on the part of the state. State structures and relationships are not exhaustive of the structures and relationships of the people within the ambit of a particular state's power. The obedience to God rather than men which the Declaration protects, relativises state power but now in a context in which collusion and distortion of their different powers by authorities of church and state may not so easily lead to Inquisition or Penal Laws. Respect for the dignity of the human person offers a more secure foundation against absolutist claims than rights of truth or some higher common good. Taken in conjunction with the growing sensitivity to human rights in general, the church's current position on religious freedom demands an understanding of state and state power which will bear some further reflection.

Because the state may not, in this view, consider itself coextensive with the rights and relationships of the people composing it, and because it has to respect the basic human dignity of these people and certain attendant rights, the state is limited by and dependent on the people, their dignity and rights. With this kind of broad political view, the state becomes the people organised for certain purposes, but not the people *tout court.* If the particular people in their full historical relationships might be described as society, the state constitutes the political aspect of society, but is not identical with society.[1] It is the society, people or community as political. The range of the political may vary enormously from very restricted to the almost unlimited of the highly bureaucratic centralised state, the one-party state or the dictatorship. The minimum limitation of range demanded by religious liberty at once resists total i.e. totalitarian claims, refuses to see the individual person as simply the subject of state power deriving his rights therefrom, and develops its traditional duality to uphold the further distinction between state and society. Whatever the terms used, this distinction is crucial to the protection of human rights and dignity in face of state power. It provides, in addition, an acceptable basis for legitimising state power, determining its range and structuring its exercise.

In the concrete situation, the distinction between state and society requires much fuller investigation. While the society might be simply described as the totality of the people with their historical relationships, the relationships are not so easily recognised, understood and evaluated. Complex questions of identity and tradition arise here, which frequently look for or influence political aspirations and solutions. The emergence of the nation-state and its continuing influence as an achievement or aspiration reveal some of the complexity of relating society and state. Attitudes to minorities or majorities and the political implications of these attitudes extend from discrimination on the basis of race or sex to treatment of people on the margins of conventional society, such as prisoners or itinerants or homosexuals. Clearly, whatever society as a whole or as a majority believes or practises may not automatically be canonised as right or legitimate for that society. That way lies the danger of a new totalitarianism. How far existing social attitudes, structures and practices may or should be given political endorsement or rejection by the state in its laws or other activities remains a continuing problem for the members of that society and their political representatives. Tricky as this problem is, it must be tackled by upholding the distinction between society, with its full sweep of human relationships and activities, and state, with its more restricted brief, derivative nature, and characteristic forms of activity such as the law. The coordinating, protective and reforming roles of law, as one important expression of the relation between society and state, will be more properly discussed later.

Society and the Church

The original duality of faith allegiance and community based on discipleship of Christ on the one hand, and political allegiance and community on the other, provides a basis for distinguishing society and state. It also provides a basis for distinguishing society as the whole historical people in the total range of their relationships, and the church as people in a relationship of faith and discipleship. Church as people is the primary understanding restored in Vatican II. In most of the societies we know, the believing people are not co-extensive in membership with the people who make up society as a whole. Even if they were, it would be a mistake to identify church and society, which includes among other dimensions the political.

The church exists in society as the community of disciples whose faith in the God of Jesus Christ assumes historical form in word and sacrament, living and worshipping, personal and structural relationships. The church cannot escape history or historical and social forms. It is within historical society that it exists and carries out its saving mission. Yet it also stands over against society, irreducible to it, challenging it, even judging it, in the world but not finally of it. The church's relationship with the political dimension of society, the state, is mediated through the historical society. With this further differentiation it becomes possible to avoid in analysis some of that reduction of church-state relations to institutional or personal power struggles which was once prevalent. The church is primarily the people in their discipleship relations and only secondarily a people structured hierarchically. This people operates as church in and through the historical society and only thereby comes in contact with society as organised politically.

Church, Kingdom and Society[2]

In analysing the socio-historical task of the church, its mission in society, it is necessary to keep in mind another duality introduced by Jesus' preaching and discipleship. The kingdom or reign of God which Jesus announced and inaugurated has already begun but is yet to be completed. The tension between historical achievement of the kingdom and eschatological fulfilment is central to any deeper understanding of church's role in history and society. The pilgrim church of sinners, which has received increasing attention of late, underlines the limits of the church's achievement at any particular time and the summons addressed to it to enter more fully into the establishment of God's reign in his world; it must be continually converted that the kingdom may be more fully at hand.

The church is not the kingdom then. It is the herald of the kingdom, the proclaimer of the Good News of the coming kingdom. In the discipleship life of its members it is at once a realisation and sign or witness of the kingdom. The church is different from but essential to kingdom as preacher, promoter and realiser at least in part. Without the church we would not know of the kingdom; we would lack the means of discerning and promoting it wherever it emerges.

'Wherever the kingdom emerges'. Not only does the kingdom exceed the church historically, in that it is always in part future, and finally eschatological, transcending history; it also exceeds it socially in the here and now. The biblical insight into the range of God's reign announced by Jesus, for example in Matthew's story of the final judgment, or Paul's discussion of the unknown God of the Athenians, or more profoundly in his analysis of the acceptance by the Gentiles of that reign through the law written in their hearts (*Rom.* 2), has developed over the centuries into a faith-understanding of human realities in history and society that recognises God's kingly power at work in diverse non-ecclesial or secular contexts.

A theology of secular realities, i.e. human but non-ecclesial entities, achievements, relationships and structures, such as language, work, medicine, law, politics, to take a random list, reveals how far the reign of God extends beyond ecclesial boundaries. This extension applies obviously to the people, with their relationships and achievements, who are not of the Christian faith and community. Vatican II's documents on non-Christian religions and on non-believers gave expression to this. More subtly and critically it applies to the non-ecclesial relationships and achievements of those within the Christian community of faith. Discerning and maintaining this duality of ecclesial and secular expressions of God's reign among Christians themselves is not easy. This is particularly so in a society where membership of the wider society is especially coextensive with that of the ecclesial or faith community, the church. Yet it is essential to true faith and a healthy society that this duality in the believer himself be not obscured or overlooked. Further reflection on and investigation into this duality is necessary to a more precise understanding of lay apostolate, social mission of the church and other contemporary growth points. For the moment it suffices to insist on the distinction between church and kingdom before returning to a consideration of the distinction and relation between historical society and kingdom.

If the church is not to be identified with the kingdom, then the society we know at any particular time more certainly is not. In some of its biblical senses 'world' may be used for the entity here called society. The term 'world' immediately suggests the ambiguity which characterises the human achievement of society understood in the context of the Christian doctrines of creation, fall and redemption. The evil which pervades society in sinful attitude, action and structure manifests itself too strikingly to allow any reflective observer to see here the best of all possible worlds. Resistance to the reign of the all-good God and loving Father of Jesus Christ is expressed in this evil and sin. 'World' and society are still subject to the redeeming love of God. His reign has begun. The evil has to be balanced by the goodness and truth, love and justice which survive and often thrive in this curiously mixed world. The problem of the good is no less puzzling in itself than the problem of evil. In a redeemed if fallen world Christian insight discerns the effects of redemption in the triumph of good over evil, in the fitful yet undeniable progress which mankind makes in realising and protecting the creative potential which belongs to God-given human dignity and is never completely obscured or eliminated by human failure.

Above all in the moral achievements of individuals and societies, but also in the aesthetic, technological and other achievements, the creative potential of mankind as realising the creative power and reign of God may be perceived, accepted and celebrated. It is for the faith-community to discern, accept, celebrate and promote the power and reign of God in history and society. In doing so, it carries out its critical social mission, and may well find an understanding and a way of action which will remove the old confusions of church action as hierarchical action, or some of the more artificial distinctions involving the apostolate of the laity. In reconsidering 'church-state' relations the intermediate realities designed to prevent confusion and improper confrontation are now more clearly evident. Distinctions of church and kingdom, of state and society, indicate how the mission of the church is in and through society in the service of the kingdom. Society operates politically in and through the state structures and personnel. Church and state do not relate directly but through the intermediate realities of kingdom and society which each respectively serves. The power struggle has to be reconceived and is certainly moved away from the eye-ball to eye-ball character which it sometimes assumed in the past. The basis and purpose of its power, in so far as one should use that term at all, must be reconsidered by the church in terms of its call to service. Too much of the recent 'service' talk about authority has had the air of cosmetic rather than real change.

The Church and Social Change

Apart from the reductionism and confusion which some earlier discussion of this topic involved, it tended to place the church in the situation of endorsing the social political *status quo,* except where directly church interests such as its religious freedom or educational interests were threatened. The duality between state and society, which the Declaration on Religious Freedom and associated teaching involve, subordinates state to society in a way that makes further freedoms possible, including the freedom to criticise and change the political *status quo.* It is only too evident today, from Russia to South Africa to Chile, that social freedoms and the associated human rights are closely intertwined with one another and demand for their healthy existence a distinction between state and society denied by totalitarian regimes of the right and the left. For reasons of expediency as well as principle, the church must resist restriction of human freedom in pursuit of its mission of discerning and establishing the kingdom in society.

In an apparently liberal society, the denial of human dignity and freedom may be more a question of society's dominance than the state's. Discrimination based on race, sex or money may even resist state efforts to remove them. Racial discrimination in North America proved stubbornly resistant to eradication by law. Attempts to resolve the Northern Ireland crisis by legal and political arrangements have shattered on the rocks of historical social attitudes and structures. A totalitarianism of society rather than state power, or at least very severe restrictions of human freedom deriving from social forces such as control of the economy, can be equally destructive of human dignity, and challenge the church in its pursuit of the kingdom by denunciation of injustice and promotion of reform.

The emerging reign of God, the summons to development which it implies, and the attracting and enabling power which it embodies, confer the ultimate capacity on society to transcend its own nature. The direction and criterion for that transformation derive also from the kingdom. Through its recognition of and commitment to the kingdom within the ambiguities of society, the church has to play a dynamic and reforming role. The pursuit of justice in society becomes, in the words of the 1971 Synod of Bishops, a constituent element of the preaching of the gospel or good news of the kingdom. Understood and exercised in this way, the social mission of the church is neither a passive acceptance of the *status quo* in return for some ecclesiastical advantage, nor an improper interference in politics.

While the church in this sense is a challenge to society, society may be no less a challenge to it. In society too, aspects of the emerging kingdom appear and take flesh. Some of these aspects may be ignored or obscured by the church itself. For all the clarity and strength of the Declaration of Religious Freedom, its message for internal church life has not been so clearly and effectively understood and implemented. In the past, the church made belated concessions to the signs of the times as signs of the kingdom. The sinfulness of the church itself diminishes its sensitivity to the coming of the kingdom, and it finds itself judged by the embodiment of the kingdom in social and secular activities and structures. The too late nineteenth-century attention to the needs of the working class may serve as a warning to such insensitivity on the part of the church and as society's judgment upon it by the standards of the kingdom.

Kingdom Values and Social Achievements

The duality between society and state demanded by the traditional duality of faith and politics or church and state and given contemporary expression in the Declaration on Religious Freedom, ensures against any reduction of social relations to legal relations, of social energy and power to state energy and power or of person to citizen with his existence and rights granted by or finally determined by the state. The social transcends the political. Society remains the source, judge and eventual transformer of the political order.

Society as a human and historical phenomenon is not exhaustive of human reality and resources. At least the historical people which constitute a particular society at a particular time are not totally expressed and bound by the relationships and structures in which they find themselves or which they have achieved at a particular time. Society is no more a closed and completed entity than the state. Its very historical character with its thrust and responsibility to the future requires that it also remain ready to transcend its present condition. Viewed as a community of persons with the free creative and finally irreducible dimension of personality, society can be seen to contain within itself this capacity and need to transform itself and its present political and legal attainments and structures.

The basis of the creativity and freedom of the person in community provokes diverse philosophical questions and answers. If they are not to collapse into closed, positivist and reductionist pseudo-answers they must transcend the historically human in some awareness of and relationship to the transhuman, the absolute or divine. For the Christian this openness to the transcendent of persons in community in history is particularised in the doctrines of creation and covenant, redemption and resurrection, summarised in the preaching of Jesus as the present and future realisation of God's kingdom with accompanying call to conversion. The kingdom, which the church as the community of Jesus' disciples is called to preach and promote, discern and realise, provides the transcendent point of reference for society's standard of achievement and the enabling power for society's self-transformation. The church as the explicitly conscious assembly of 'kingdom-spotters' has the responsibility in and to society of discerning and applying kingdom standards, of encouraging and releasing kingdom energies. It is in discharge of this responsibility that it impinges through society on the political community or state.

To speak of the standards of the kingdom as applicable to social life is to raise a number of difficult issues at once. In its full and proper sense the kingdom is not of this world. It cannot be identified or realised in historical terms. Its ultimate transcendence takes it beyond historical realisation, precise definition or even adequate conceptualisation. It has not entered because it cannot enter into the heart of man to conceive what this kingdom to be shared by God with man will be like. Yet the kingdom or reign of God preached by Jesus *is,* here and now, if only as a shadowy reflection of the ultimate reality. Wherever human beings in their persons and communities are recognised, respected and cared for as irreducible centres of knowledge and freedom, love and creativity, as images of God and children of the Father in Christian terms, there is Christ at work in his saving and transforming role, there the kingly rule of his Father is emerging.

The values of the kingdom which seek historical embodiment in the structures, attitudes and activities of society have at once the transcendent reference of the kingdom and the incarnate reference of history. They are expressed in the human moral achievements of and struggle for peace, freedom, justice and human fulfilment, while at the same time they retain their character as gifts and challenges of the kingly rule of God. Social ethics as discovered and implemented in history mediates for a particular historical society these kingdom values. It is in discovering, teaching and realising the demands of social ethics that the church contributes to the emergence of kingdom values in society.

The possibilities and limitations of this church task have to be taken seriously. With its central reference points of Jesus and the kingdom the church has a perspective and a standard by which these values can be more fully understood and finally tested. However, acceptance of Jesus and the kingdom does not automatically provide moral insight into the extended and complex range of social structures, relationships, attitudes and activities which constitute the life of a particular society at a particular time, let alone the lives of all the societies of all times. There is patient learning work to be done here and the church must apply itself to it conscientiously. That it is a slow learner in these matters history abundantly illustrates. The long acceptance of the institution of slavery or of racial and sexist discrimination are powerful reminders of the limitations of the church in search of kingdom values.

And it is clearly not just a question of time and effort. The church itself in its sinful condition can be blind to the true demands of the incoming kingdom. It may and does put its own institutional survival ahead of the respect and care for all people, particularly the oppressed, which are the true signs of the kingdom. So much of the struggle of the past between church and state was often dictated by considerations of institutional power rather than protection and promotion of kingdom values. To be fair and accurate these kingdom values were seen as being contained within the confines of the church.

Kingdom values emerge also beyond the church and it is the responsibility of the church to help discern, promote and realise them. In fulfilling this task the church has to realise that in its own structures, attitudes and activities it stands under the judgment of the kingdom and its values. It too shares the ambiguity of history and the sinful condition of humankind. Not only may it selfishly confine its interests to church realities but these realities may even in their sinfulness be countersigns of the kingdom or signs of the anti-kingdom. Absence of justice, truth, freedom and compassion in the church subject it to the condemnation of the kingdom and leave it in a very weak position to confront the wider society in the kingdom's name. Again, church history, universal and local, offers painful reminders of how church authorities and structures have violated the standards of the kingdom and obscured its values. Without a continuing consciousness of this and a constant effort at conversion and reform the church's mission to society in service of the kingdom will appear hypocritical and be seriously undermined. The beam in the church's eye can sometimes create more blindness to the true nature of the kingdom and its values than the mote in society's.

The church's services to the kingdom in society is a collaborative one both in discerning and in promoting these values. The values have to be discovered, preserved and developed in history. In this the church provides its own source of wisdom but in interaction with other traditions of moral understanding. The historical character of moral truth does not simply relativise it but allows for progressive discovery and clarification. As society changes in history, moral demands and their understanding change. The church is part of the movement of history and strives to purify and develop its moral understanding with the aid of other currents of moral reflection and insight. It performs a critical and discriminating task but in a basically learning stance, sharing the fruits of its own learning process with wider society and drawing in turn on society's achievements. Moral values of the kingdom are not the preserve of the church and its tradition. It has much to learn from other traditions as well as much to offer.

In the task of promoting kingdom values as distinct from discerning them, the church must also and as people cooperate with the groups and movements of the wider society engaged in this work. This will sometimes mean initiating work totally neglected. And in the fields of education and health care, for example, the church has an honourable tradition in this respect particularly through the work of its religious orders. That work is still necessary, although its innovatory character might be renewed so that as particular values and concerns receive adequate attention otherwise, church bodies seek out the neglected or undiscovered needs of peoples. In developing countries as they develop, politically and economically, the church people must be particularly sensitive to the people who will inevitably be missed out. The traditional church stance of *control* for the sake of service also needs revision. Cooperation with other service groups and structures by the church should be concerned with how far the values are promoted and realised, not with who enjoys control. Of course the way forward for the realisation of kingdom values is not direct and easy. Unjust principalities and powers with their demonic values will frequently triumph. The church must be in the forefront in discerning, denouncing, protesting and opposing this destructive counter-kingdom. With its basic reference point in Jesus Christ it has the source of light and strength and the model of response in confronting social sin and evil. The exorcism of these demonic powers and the overcoming of this evil will be no less costly for the church than for its master. In history, the way of the kingdom under the sign of sin is for Jesus' disciples the way of the Cross. That is the final extent of their commitment to serving the kingdom in society.

Human Rights

In discerning and promoting the values of the kingdom the present awareness of and concern for human rights has remarkable significance. Retracing the steps of this chapter to the duality introduced by Christian faith and community, with the implication of religious freedom, one came to recognise the further duality of society and state. That duality is critical to the emergence of human rights of which religious freedom is in some ways a paradigmatic expression. With such freedom the competence of the state is restricted and persons in the wider society remain open to and transcend political authorities with their final call to obey God rather than men. That space between society and state has developed in political philosophy and practice in the last couple of centuries to the point where a Universal Declaration of Human Rights by the UN in 1948 and subsequent International Covenants and Conventions have made concrete the freedoms and claims inextricably linked with the human person in society.

All this is consistent with and indeed demanded by the creation-incarnation-eschatological understanding of person as subject of faith and justice in chapter one. Indeed, the inviolability, freedom, fairness and participation due to each person in society, as outlined there, provide a convenient first stage in elaborating and expounding the somewhat untidy lists of civil and political, social, cultural and economic rights presented in the international documents.

The inviolability of the person, which enables him to transcend state laws and authority and find his final significance in creation and incarnation, leads quickly and easily into a whole range of rights as protections or immunities. They range from the very basic rights to life and bodily integrity to freedom from arbitrary arrest, detention, torture, and to the right to privacy. Such rights are freedoms in the sense of immunities, involving the right not to be interfered with or hindered by others. In that sense all rights might be considered under the rubric of freedom with its demand for social space in movement, expression, association and so on. Such rights may be broadly classified as civil and political.

With fairness and participation one is moving into the area of claims rather than immunities — that is, a claim on a positive response from society and resources rather than simply immunity from interference by society. There is more (but not exclusive) concern with economic and social rights. Fairness in distribution of goods and services makes clear demands on resources and has obvious economic implications but it is also a matter of political policy, decision and organisation. This is evident in the welfare provisions of the modern society and in the new attention to rights (as claims) to work, to a minimum wage, to more just trade and aid arrangements.

Participation in shaping one's life and destiny, in decisions affecting these, makes political and economic claims which are denied to the person at the cost of his real personhood. It is only through such participation that he becomes a personal subject in society, not simply an object of social and historical forces or a unit under state control. The development and protection of peoples as subjects of their own history, personal and social, is the true goal of human rights legislation and its implementations. It is another expression of the coming of the kingdom and its values. It represents therefore a fresh formulation of the church's call to serve the kingdom in society.

In their historical emergence and acceptance human rights constitute a particular expression of kingdom values. They are, however, still being discovered as well as needing further implementation. Human rights have not been handed down from heaven and are in need of revision and refinement in their range and expression. So, while the western tradition took easily to the developing expression of political and civil rights, a great deal more difficulty arises in regard to the social and economic spheres. What is the meaning of the right to work for instance? How should it be legislated for? Against whom should it be vindicated in the courts?

For all the further work necessary to a comprehensive and systematic understanding of human rights there can be no doubt of their critical role in the future development of mankind. In particular, while the social and economic rights are least understood and implemented, their unbreakable unity with civil and political rights must be maintained. Above all, distinctions between types of rights should not be used to impugn the record in the field of human rights of one's opponents, and to excuse one's own. The failures today in first, second and third world and in their structured relations to implement all manner of rights are much too serious for political point-scoring or evasive arguments *ad homines*. The understanding of human rights may still be incomplete; it is, however, far ahead of implementation.

The creation-incarnation dimension of human rights might be well described in relation to the inbreaking kingdom or reign of God. These rights are signs of that kingdom, hints of the transcendent and eschatological breaking through the social and historical. In the insight they provide into human dignity and the way they embody respect for it, they realise, however partially and obscurely, the fullness awaiting humankind in the final kingdom. They are anticipations as well as signs of the kingdom. It is as such that they demand the concern of the church and enter its mission of service to the kingdom, a service which as I noted earlier will depend for its effectiveness not only on the understanding and commitment of the church as community but also on its respect for and protection of these human rights in its own structures and relationships.[3]

Political Change and Liberation Theology

The evidence for the presence of the kingdom in society is incomplete, obscure and ambiguous. The social evil inherited from the past, endorsed in the present and projected into the future is not so easily overcome. Indeed it was in the darkness and near despair of Calvary, with the apparently final triumph of the forces of evil in the death of Jesus, that these powers were definitively overcome. But their residual force remains and the glorious coming of the kingdom must, like the resurrection of Jesus, transcend history. What is achieved in history is always partial and always at risk. Kingdom, redemption and salvation seek historical expression but cannot achieve historical completion. That historical expression is increasingly understood in a social and political sense and not just in terms of personal salvational grace in history and ultimate salvation in eternity. The new life given in history affects humankind more and more in all its historical and social dimensions. That new life is diminished and distorted by the diminishing and distorting structures whereby millions of men are deprived of their human rights, denied access to kingdom values, and prevented from becoming the subjects of their own history. The theological movement which has made its own the meaning and removal of such privation and denial and oppression is known as liberation theology. In any attempt to understand the mind of the believing community in today's sin-laden society, the insights of liberation theology are of particular significance.

Rise of Liberation Theology

The theology of liberation[4] originated in Latin America

in the late sixties and early seventies. It is a fresh theological attempt to understand the salvation achieved in Jesus Christ in historical and social terms. In face of appalling social, economic and political oppression throughout the continent, bishops and theologians had to ask themselves anew what could salvation mean and how could it be achieved for the oppressed masses. They no longer felt able to accept salvation outside society and history as adequate to the meaning and demand of the gospel in their situation. While the fullness of salvation might lie beyond history in the kingdom yet to come, in Jesus' own words the kingdom was also at hand in the here and now at least as promise and summons. The grace of that promise and the task of that summons should be understood in the salvation of the oppressed by their liberation from the social, economic and political slavery in which they found themselves. St Paul's freedom for which Christ has set men free concerns this historical enslavement to the sinful structures of this world. The God of Jesus Christ as the God of Abraham and Moses is a God who acts in history to set his people free. His people are above all the poor, the deprived and the oppressed. Mary rejoiced at the coming of the Saviour because God had shown his power by putting down the mighty from their thrones and exalting the lowly, filling the hungry with good things and sending the rich empty away. And Jesus announced his mission in Nazareth by applying to himself and his mission the words of the prophet Isaiah: 'The Spirit of the Lord is upon me because he has appointed me to preach the good news to the poor. He has sent me to proclaim release to the captives and recovering of sight to the blind, to set at liberty those who are oppressed, to proclaim the acceptable year of the Lord'. And these were the signs which he gave to John the Baptist's messengers when John sent to enquire if he really were the Messiah. The God who had led his people out of the slavery of Egypt had finally sent his own Son to be the definitive liberator of his people.

Much of this may seem conventional and traditional enough, and so it is. Genuinely Christian theology derives from a tradition and a community, the church. Yet genuine theology undergoes powerful changes as it seeks to understand and implement the gospel message in different historical circumstances. The circumstances of oppression in Latin America were not entirely new but the perception of them in terms of analysis of their causes, and of a vision for their transformation combined with a commitment to that transformation, disclosed an understanding of salvation as involving historical liberation and the struggle for it in a new and compelling way. The first official endorsement of this understanding came from the Conference of Latin American Bishops meeting at Medellin in 1968. Their next meeting in January 1979 confirmed the general orientation of Medellin. The theology of liberation, however, developed very significantly in the next ten years. The engagement of laity, priest;, religious and even bishops in the struggle for liberation has intensified, only to be matched by increasing and brutal resistance from the oppressors, politicial and economic.

In the same decade liberation theology spread to other underdeveloped and oppressed regions. African and Asian theologians are developing their own theology in their own circumstances but clearly inspired by the Latin American movement. In the developed world various deprived groups have adapted this theology to their own conditions, notably black American theologians and feminist theologians. Despite its apparent exotic origins the theology of liberation has much to offer Christians in every country. As a way of understanding and living the gospel it has many fruitful ideas and practices, not the least fruitful of which is that practices are more important than ideas and provide a better starting point for theological reflection. This relation between reflection and practice with its Marxist associations and the connected emphasis on the role of social analysis in theology will continue to affect the doing of theology for decades to come. I want to concentrate on one typical expression of this, found in some liberation theologians: the historical context of liberation and its thrust towards enabling person and community to become the subjects rather than the objects of their history. Not only is it a fruitful insight in itself, but it seems to me to have special relevance to the Rhodesian situation and so is deserving of particular attention here.

Subjects and Objects of History

Jesus' message of repentance and conversion and Paul's exposition of this in terms of freedom or liberation from sin, death and the law, extends in terms of liberation theology to social, political and economic conversion and liberation. While Exodus reveals effectively the societal dimensions of God's activity in history, it is with the fulfilment of this activity as manifest in Jesus Christ that as Christians, liberation theologians are necessarily and predominantly concerned.

The social, political and economic conditions in which so many people live demand conversion if they are to enjoy historically any of the freedom of Jesus Christ. To speak as if this freedom could be entirely displaced beyond history ('pie in the sky') is to ignore its full meaning, render its comfortable preachers hypocritical and endorse the Marxist critique of religion as opium for the people. The process of conversion and liberation deriving from Jesus Christ must reach people in the full dimensions of their slavery. Release from that slavery, however partial, enables people to become subjects of their own history rather than objects. They acquire the freedom and resources to shape their own lives and reach for their own destiny. In slavery they are but the object of forces over which they have no control, ensnared by structures which they do not operate and cannot amend. Such enslavement may so marginalise people that they become total objects, non-persons, really absent from history. Their degree of enslavement may vary but their right to liberation in the name of Christ and the Christian's duty to respond seem well founded.

Becoming a subject in history, able to perceive and choose one's way of life, forms no more than a fresh expression of the traditional Christian understanding of the human person. More deeply still it must be presupposed in the whole theology of faith as free personal response to divine personal call within history. Only human subject can meet divine subject in faith. The denial of a person's subject condition denies in varying degrees his freedom and ability to encounter and respond in faith to the ultimate Subject. Of course people may and do triumph over the most adverse conditions from Gulag to Auschwitz, from the barrios of Latin America to the Tribal Trust Lands of Rhodesia to affirm their subjectivity and maintain their faith. Personal and communal liberation, subjectivity and faith are not simply dependent on or reducible to political, social and economic freedom. Yet these freedoms are demanded by the call to liberation, subjectivity and faith. The denial or reduction of them diminishes or may destroy any incarnate subjectivity and so restrict the possibility of Christian faith. The absence of basic liberation contradicts the thrust of evangelisation. The exercise of evangelisation involves the work of liberation.

The obviously enslaved are the poor, the deprived, the discriminated against and the marginalised. They cry to heaven, if not for vengeance, at least for liberation for themselves and conversion for their oppressors. In truth the oppressors are also enslaved. But it is a comfortable slavery anaesthetised by the drugs of wealth and power, abundance of goods and services. They are in need of liberation also, but unaware for the most part of that need. Dives, in his enslavement, is not easily awakened from his postprandial slumber, not even by the cries of Lazarus at the gate. The rude awakening that is to come may be too late for the historical liberation of either Dives or Lazarus. In the story Lazarus operates as the potential liberator. His own starving condition may not be ignored by himself, and his cries might have released Dives just a little from his self-imposed imprisonment and enslavement to the goods of the world.

The parable has far-reaching implications. The poor and deprived as more easily alerted by their needs to the injustice and slavery rampant in the world are the obvious liberators, not just of themselves as oppressed but also of their oppressors. Indeed in the light of God's activity in Jesus Christ, liberation is a gift before it is an achievement, a gift from the ultimate Other, the Father, but mediated in history through human others, our neighbours. The process of liberation, of setting free, of becoming subjects of history is a mutual process. The oppressor cannot be liberated on his own or by himself. His subjectivity is an intersubjectivity and is given and achieved in the mutual exchange of neighbour love as it derives from and expresses divine love. Even within the Godhead subjectivity is intersubjectivity; divine freedom expresses the loving and exchange of the three divine persons. In history human subjectivity and freedom emerge and flourish in loving relationships and liberating structures by which men encounter one another in freedom, justice and peace. The social conversion which is necessary for this is basically a conversion of person to person, sex to sex, class to class and race to race. Such conversion demands and is expressed in radical structural change right through the social, political and economic worlds. Such conversion is demanded by Jesus' original preaching and is the gateway for the fuller emergence of the kingdom of his Father.

Liberation and conversion are not cheaply available. The death and renunciation of Jesus Christ provide an index of the cost. It is a death and renunciation, a conversion not only of a personal but of a communal kind to which people are summoned. It will bear hardly on Dives and his friends, although it has to be realised that they have been enjoying their comforts while Lazarus and his much greater number of friends have been denied even the crumbs.

The scope of this vision is frightening as well as exciting. The danger is that it will taper off in so much religious rhetoric and sound so utopian as to be easily ignored. That is why the liberation theologians insist on hard-headed social, political and economic analysis as an integral part of their theological enterprise. At this stage, the theological going becomes much more difficult. A variety of analyses from the social sciences are available. Political analyists can differ greatly and so can economists. There is the further difficulty of the voiced or unvoiced ideology or political and social vision which informs all such analyses. The neutral social analyst has long been exposed as a myth. For many of the Latin Americans the problem is solved by consciously adopting and seeming to justify some form of Marxian analysis. Other liberation theologians there and elsewhere find this approach unacceptable. It must be admitted, however, that some elements of Marx's teaching and of the social philosophies and sciences influenced by his ideas appear to affect most liberation theologies in third world countries. How far this creates problems for them as Christians or solves problems for them as liberationists demands separate treatment.

Christians and Socialism[5]

In many areas of the world including Rhodesia and South Africa one of the major fears of the church and state leaders is the danger of a socialist take-over. It is usually expressed in fact in terms of a communist or even Russian take-over. Immediately one is faced with the confusion of terms, sometimes deliberate, in which this debate is conducted. To equate for example a socialist government in Britain or Sweden with that in Russia — or even a communist government in Chile with that in East Germany — is similar to equating parliamentary government in South Africa with that in Holland or the presidential role in France or the United States with that in Yugoslavia or Argentina. There are as many brands of socialism in theory and practice as there are of capitalism, democracy or liberalism. Indeed socialism is frequently used as a denial or contradiction of one or other of these three distinct ideas, traditions and practices, and sometimes of all three. The confusion is further compounded, and dishonestly so, when any criticism of or threat to the status quo by a deprived group or race is branded socialist or communist when its inspiration and programme is simply basic justice or national independence. To equate movements for social justice, racial equality or national independence with communist subversion is the easy way to justify a national security ideology which increases oppression and prepares the way for a possible eventual explosion. I have no doubt that such confusion and dishonesty has played its role in Rhodesia, for example, in making war practically unavoidable.

The difficulties for Christians reach further and deeper, however, at both the theoretical and the practical level. At both levels the really serious question for Christians is how far socialism is atheistic in its belief and destructive of religion in its exercise. At this stage of world history it is clear that many socialists and socialisms are neither atheistic nor opposed to religion. The experience of socialist governments in many countries of Western Europe and elsewhere bears that out. It is not sufficient to say: but of course the problem is Marxist Socialism or Marxist-Leninism or Communism or Soviet Communism. All forms of socialism are historically and philosophically dependent on Marx, his analysis and his programme. How far they have transcended or deviated from or disagree about the true interpretation of Marx and his collaborator or successors provides enormous scope for debate, in particular on the relationship between socialism and religion.

Christianity and Socialism

In the aftermath of John XXIII (*Mater et Magistra*), Vatican II (*Gaudium et Spes*) and Paul VI (*Populorum Progressio*), it is clear that forms of socialism simply as political and economic programmes designed to promote national and international justice do not conflict with basic Christian faith. They may be much more in harmony with Christian faith and morality than many of the forms of capitalism of which the popes and other church leaders have become increasingly critical.

The key question remains: are there forms of socialist theory and practice which are incompatible with Christian faith and practice? The answer is certainly yes. Like other forms of socialism they derive from Marxism. Are they the really Marxist Socialism? In other words is Marxist Socialism, or its varieties as defended and promoted by Marxists, incompatible with Christian faith and freedom? A large body of Marxist literature and decades of Marxist governmental practice suggest an unqualified yes.

There are, however, some further nuances of the debate. One can discern developments in Marxist thinking and practice that make it less antagonisitic to religion and Christianity. The Marxist-Christian dialogue in Britain, Central Europe and Latin America as well as the historic compromise between

Christian Democrats and the Communist party in Italy, and the various alliances against oppression and exploitation in Latin America, show how people and times and ideologies are changing. Such dialogue and collaboration were already indicated in John XXIII's encyclical, *Mater et Magistra.*

At the theological level the dialogue has reached its fullest expression in the emergence of Latin American liberation theology. How far such theologians endorse or require Marxist social and economic analysis in their theological work is not always clear. Some certainly do endorse that analysis whether it is a requirement of their theology or not. How far they may legitimately do this while avoiding the reductionist politics, philosophy and atheism of many of their sources and mentors, it is difficult to say. Given the current movement in Marxist thinking itself these Christians hope that the exchange will not be all one way and that the distinctions they draw between social and economic analysis and reductionist philosophy or ideology will be appreciated by Marxists also. Even if these distinctions are not recognised or respected, may Christians collaborate in resisting the immediate and overwhelming oppression of an exploiting group backed up by a national security ideology no less abhorrent to Christianity? To put it another way: may Christians, in discharge of their obligation to denounce and resist a clearly unchristian regime, accept the help of people whose ultimate ideology is also suspect? The dilemma may become even more acute. However, its clear presentation should reveal any bias in favour of one clearly oppressive and immoral group as against another prospectively oppressive group. It is in such difficult situations that hard decisions have to be made. Refusal to decide or lack of action for justice are not legitimate merely because others in search of justice in the situation have suspect credentials.

In the African context, particularly in Southern Africa, further practical considerations apply. The influence and ambitions of the Soviet Union and its allies are a factor. And their record in terms of human freedoms, including religious freedom, is fairly clear. Yet the Africans are not to be regarded as simply naïve in this respect. They know the imperialist and repressive record of the Soviet Union. Their use of arms and training facilities supplied by Soviet Russia and other communist countries was in some cases their only option, and does not necessarily commit them to Russian policy or control later. Their espousal of Marxist policy may be at least tactical, to ensure continued Marxist support. They have on their own continent the inspiration and practical example of an African socialism which respects human rights and religion in the Ujaama movement of President Nyerere of Tanzania.[6] In the struggle for independence and justice his words and achievements seem more convincingly Christian than the record of the white colonial racist and capitalist regimes which have prevailed so long without too much Christian criticism and opposition. In the ambiguous world in which we live it is not always easy to tell friend from foe. Continuing discrimination and shifting alliances will be called for in the pursuit of justice. Christians and Socialists will often be seeking to overcome together manifest injustices. What replaces these injustices will have its own limitations. It is the duty of Christians to ensure that the new structures reflect kingdom values such as justice and freedom and protect the dignity and worth of all members of society by upholding the distinction between society and state and monitoring its observance. Common ownership of the means of production and other economic features will be assessed according to the needs of the people and the promotion of these values.

3.

Politics and Violence in
Christian Perspective

An early decision for this project was to treat the question of political violence in the broader context of political structures, political justice and political change. Without that context writer and reader could be too easily entrapped in such a narrow debate about violent incidents and comparative atrocities that the underlying structure and moral evaluation of violence used in defence of the established order, or to undermine it, would escape discussion and analysis. Much of the denunciation of one state's violence against another or of 'revolutionary' violence by 'law and order' supporters, and of 'law and order' violence by 'revolutionary' supporters, confines itself to unexamined assumptions about the justice of one side and the injustice and immoral violence of the other. The tragic history of political violence, inter-state and intra-state, reveals innumerable examples of this type of 'dialogue of the deaf'. It is evidently operative in Northern Ireland, the Middle East and Southern Africa today, to mention just a few contemporary illustrations. Unless political violence is analysed in relation to politics it is impossible to offer any moral evaluation of it or to respond to it in a moral and effective way.

The moral analysis here is within a Christian perspective for a Christian community. This will, it is hoped, not make it any less moral in its conclusions or any less rigorous in its analysis. It will be taking account, however, of the special responsibilities of the church community, its members and its leaders, to the political community and its well-being, and so of the violence which may disrupt that community and destroy its well-being. The relationships between Christian community and the existing or aspiring political community, already discussed, provide the appropriate setting for this further stage in the discussion.

Preliminary Questions

In addition to the earlier extensive discussions of faith, justice, church and politics, there are certain other preliminaries that need to be mentioned here, though any adequate discussion of them would vastly exceed the limits and scope of this work. The pervasiveness of human violence, both domestic and political, can be readily recognised in the historical and contemporary world. This is not to say that violence is inevitable either in domestic or political life. It is merely to record the fact that most nations and many families have experienced violence in defence or pursuit of particular goals. Concerned as I am with political violence, I find myself occasionally exposed to the patronising racist remarks of white people in Africa about tribal wars which devastated Africa before the advent of the white man and are liable to do so again after his departure. I can only look sadly at my own country Ireland, my continent Europe or the Great Plains of the United States where I write this and consider the history of violence in those places in all its tribal, national and even genocidal scope. The West has a lot to teach and has taught a lot to the rest of the world about the political significance of violence and its increasing technological capacity. But in the history of humankind it is difficult for any group or nation to take a self-righteous stand on its superiority to and detachment from the violent ways of others.

The reasons for such widespread and continuing violence between people in search of political benefits may be illuminated by various studies, ethological of animals, fish and birds by people like Konrad Lorenz, psychological and sociological by people like Freud or Marx or Erich Fromm, or theological by a host of writers from Augustine to Karl Barth. Yet it would be a brave if scarcely a wise man, who would attempt to synthesise such a vast array of material and offer a final, definitive answer to the question of the causes of human aggression, violence and war in preparation for a possible final, definitive solution to this recurring threat to human society and human living.

The aim of this chapter is much more modest. I will, of course, be confining myself to political violence, that is, to use a working definition, the deliberate destruction of human health, life and property in pursuit of a political good. The character of such violence as widespread in human history does not necessarily lead to pessimism and defeatism or to the paralysing despair or escape expressed in the belief 'that there is nothing to be done'. We do, however, need a sobering realism in the discussion. Most states we know of either came into existence through war or have otherwise engaged in war or at least been compelled to use actual coercion or threat of war to maintain their existence. Distinctions should and will be made as to the goals and kinds of violence employed but its close and apparently necessary association with achieving or retaining political power, as with maintaining law and order, should be honestly recognised if one is to have a realistic view of the problem. Such realism may father a further humility in analyses attempting to understand and evaluate a particular violent situation such as Rhodesia, and in participants, observers and reporters as they try to understand what is going on around them and why. Without such humility, analysis, participation and even observation too easily become blindly partisan. This then reinforces the violence by reinforcing the misunderstanding, mistrust and deception that is already fuelling it.

At this stage of analysis I will be trying to examine the various kinds of political violence and their various motivations on different sides of a dispute, with a view to providing some insight into the moral evaluation and personal response demanded of Christians. At a later stage, in part two, I will be attempting to understand the basically diverse strands in the Rhodesian struggle with the same object in mind for Rhodesian Christians.

I do not wish to become embroiled in the thorny theoretical question of whether there is a specifically Christian morality or whether in this or other moral issues Christians share exactly the same moral view for the same reasons as non-Christians. Elsewhere I have tried to show that this may be a misstatement of the problem. But all that would simply take me too far afield here. Yet certain clarifications are called for.

I am concerned with Christian understanding of and Christian response to the problem of political violence. Within thought and history one may distinguish two major traditions which might be described as 'the just war' tradition and the 'pacifist' tradition, although both terms are apt to be seriously misleading. The fuller discussion to come will remove the ambiguities in terminology. Here I wish to make the point that both traditions call on distinctive Christian arguments, particularly drawn from the teaching of Jesus and the New Testament but both also invoke at critical stages of development what one might call non-religious moral arguments and certainly non-Christian moral arguments. Both enjoy the favour and disfavour of Christians and non-Christians, for religious and non-religious reasons. It is certainly not possible to settle the specifically Christian ethic debate, if it can be settled at all, by appealing to the paradigmatic case of political violence. And it is equally impossible, at least within the Catholic and many other Christian traditions, to settle the morality of all types of political violence by invoking Christian faith and its sources. Again, the preliminary difficulties sketched here may encourage a modesty in moral analysis and judgment that could lead to more effective response in word and deed in particular situations.

To end this preliminary section I wish to make clear again that I am writing primarily out of the Catholic tradition for a Catholic community. Christians do not divide along denominational lines on many of these issues, although the 'church-sect' distinction popularised in America by Ernest Troetsch has led to some characterisations which may in the world today be seen as inadequate. Allowing for this historical complication, what I have to say will I hope be accessible and acceptable to Christians of many traditions, although I am well aware that it may be inaccessible and certainly unac-

ceptable to some Christians in my own tradition, the Catholic.
I hope that it will be read in the spirit in which it was written,
as an effort to plot a way for Catholic Christian disciples
through the very tangled jungle of faith, politics and violence.

The Two Traditions[2]

Although the very significant work of Roland H. Bainton,
Christian Attitudes Towards Peace and War (New York
1960), distinguished three attitudes to war or political
violence associated with 'just war theory', the crusades and
pacifism, I will speak of two traditions or tendencies or poles
within Christian history. In crude terms these traditions or
tendencies have sometimes been distinguished by their
acceptance of war and political violence in certain defined
circumstances or their rejection of them in any circumstances.
The first has been conventionally labelled the 'just war
position'; the second the pacifist or non-violent or alternative
position. While the historical origins and theological justifications of these two positions are more complex than is usually
admitted, there is considerable truth in the view that the
second or 'pacifist' position was the dominant one among
Christians prior to the Constantinian recognition of the church
and that the 'just war' position has been the dominant one
since. Athenagoras in his *A Plea for Christians* (177 A.D.),
Tertullian (*c.* 155–*c.* 240) in various writings, Origen (*c.* 185
–254) and Lactantius (*c.* 250–*c.* 280) defend Christians in
their loyalty to the Empire despite their objection to military
service. They base their appeal on the teaching and example
of Jesus except for Lactantius who proposes a 'natural law'
defence of pacifism.

The 'Just War' Tradition

In the aftermath of the decree of Constantine (313),
Ambrose (*c.* 339–397) and Augustine (354–430) effectively initiated a quite different tradition in which the
responsibility of Christians to serve the Empire militarily
was defended and the outlines of a just war theory appeared.
The fuller development of this theory had to await the

theological explosion of the scholastic period. Aquinas made his contribution but the highpoint of development came with Francis of Vitoria (1483–1546) who was one of the original thinkers and promoters in the field of international law.

The 'just war' position continued to receive support among Christian leaders, and further theological development on both sides of the Reformation division as well as philosophical elaboration from figures as diverse as the Dutchman philosopher of law, Hugo Grotius (1583–1645) and English philosopher John Locke (1633–1704). The early nineteenth-century theorist of war, von Clausewitz, moved decisively beyond the 'just war' criteria. With the work of Hegel and Marx the strictly ethical character of the argument about political violence, in both philosophy and theology, was subsumed into wider considerations of philosophy of history that basically separates it from the just war tradition. Later analyses of violence as glorifying or emancipating of itself, by writers like Georges Sorel and Frantz Fanon, are still further removed from 'just war' analysts and defenders. And it would be a distortion of the truth to see such analyses as more or less consistent developments of the original acceptance of violence as being sometimes justified, an acceptance which grew into the 'just war' theory. However, adherents and defenders of the just war theory themselves succumbed to exploring the opening for 'moral violence' provided by the just war position more often than they rejected the restraint it was intended to impose. While deferring to the theory of Vitoria, with all its requirements of just cause, last resort and just means, the statesmen, soldiers and even churchmen have followed a very different practice. It would be difficult to point to a war in which these requirements were all convincingly fulfilled, but easy to point to churchmen and statesmen who passionately claimed they were. World War I and World War II provide instructive contrasts in this regard. World War I is now commonly regarded as unjustified whether in its causes or as last resort, yet the attitudes of the contending powers and their churches with their chaplains, their reassuring justifications, acceptance of the glorification of war and even of the fomenting of hatred of the enemy, make sorry reading now. The sermon by the Anglican Bishop of London in 1915 is typical of hundreds:

> . . . to save the freedom of the world, everyone who loves freedom and honour, everyone who puts principle before ease and life before mere living, is banded in a great crusade — we cannot deny it — to kill Germans, to kill them not for the sake of killing, but to save the world, to kill the young as well as the old, to kill those who have shown kindness to our wounded as well as those who crucified the Canadian soldier, who sank the Lusitania, and who turned the machine guns on the civilians of Aerschot and Louvain; and to kill them lest civilisation itself be killed.[3]

The high regard for the justice of the Allied cause in World War II is still, by and large, unchallenged. Yet the cause to be defended had little enough to do with the immediate occasion of the war, the invasion of Poland which was lost in the peace anyway; still less to do with the protection of the Jews, known even before the war to be under threat, and destined to lose six million in the concentration camps before the end of the war. Indeed the failure of the Allies to bomb the railroads to Auschwitz, and the refusal of the British to assist in the evacuation of Jews as well as the means later adopted of area bombing at enormous civilian cost to the enemy and military cost to the Allies, capped by the atomic bombings of Hiroshima and Nagasaki, and the pursuit of the war to unconditional surrender, must throw considerable doubt on the justice of that war. The justice of the means used were seriously called in question at the time of the area bombing, by Bishop Bell of Chichester and American moral theologian John Forde, SJ. Recent moral commentary has been more severe on the decision to use 'unconditional surrender' as the only ending of the war, in the light of the 'last resort' criterion, while the moral qualifying of the objective causes and subjective intentions of the Allies gathers momentum.

More significant for the practical applicability of the 'just war' theory are some more general trends of the nineteenth and twentieth centuries. The development of the Geneva and the Hague Conventions in the nineteenth century with regard, for example, to non-combatants and prisoners of war and, later on, the use of weapons such as gas, constituted particular refinements of the 'just means' criterion. They were directed towards the 'humanisation' or 'civilisation' of war; taken in another way they were seen as inevitable expressions of power struggles and imperial expansion. In this context it seemed that the 'just cause' criterion was being abandoned in the face of the inevitability of war between the great powers and the best that could be hoped for was not the avoidance of war but the limitation of its means or its effects.

Some of that respect for limits persevered through World War I and World War II but it was steadily eroded. As von Clausewitz had noted in his classic work *On War* (1832), the means tend to expand to secure the proposed end at whatever cost. Some of that expansion was already evident both in the ground warfare and in the introduction of aerial warfare in World War I. The expansion accelerated in World War II as I have indicated. And with the advent of atomic bombs and nuclear warfare the whole possibility of a just war was open to question, given the indiscriminate, uncontrollable and, perhaps, finally annihilating character of the means.

Despite the existence of these means they have not, in their most extreme form, yet been used in war. Indeed some people claim that their existence has contributed to world peace by a kind of mutual terror. The many wars which have occurred since World War II have been limited in at least not using atomic or nuclear weapons. Otherwise, such limitation as, for example, observing the criterion of just means or the nineteenth-century conventions, has scarcely been conspicuous from Algeria to the Middle East to Vietnam.

The third major problem of the 'just war' theory derives from the character of most recent wars: in terms of cause, from one point of view, wars of national liberation, and in terms of means, guerrilla wars.

The cause of national liberation from domestic or foreign tyranny is not new to the 'just war' tradition although it creates some problems for it. Tyrannicide as distinct from sedition was justified in particular circumstances by St Thomas Aquinas and does provide the basis for developing a justification for rebellion against a tyrannical government provided all the other criteria are satisfied. The obviously difficult case of the declaration of war by legitimate authority must be applied in an interpretative way. Let us suppose that the formal government has lost its authority which then reverts to the people on whose behalf the rebels declare war. The rejection of the existing 'law and order' makes it difficult but not impossible to claim that the 'war' will not lead to greater evil than already exists. This depends on the degree of evil which already exists and what the hopes of success in overcoming it are.

The churches have in the past been much less sympathetic to rebellion against the established order or war of liberation, than to interstate wars in which their own state was involved. This was undoubtedly based on a conserving attitude to the current order and hope of its peaceful reform, judgment coloured by the relations between leaders of the church and leaders of the existing order. Where they were in total opposition, as in the case of Pope Pius V and Queen Elizabeth I of England, a rather different attitude prevailed. That attitude was neatly confirmed in the case of one of Elizabeth's successors, William of Orange, only in this case the Pope supported the foreign and Protestant intruder William against the incumbent and Catholic James. Self-interest and self-service have played a significant role in the judgment of churches and churchmen in all wars, and especially in their predominantly negative judgments on wars of revolt. Irish history offers frequent evidence of this. When the majority of wars tend to be wars of rebellion against the established order, fresh difficulties arise for the 'just war' theory and its Christian interpreters.

The Alternative or 'Pacifist' Tradition

It is difficult to find a suitable description for that Christian attitude to war which rejects or transcends that of the 'just war'. 'Pacifist', even when it is not understood simply as 'passivist', does not do justice to the diverse people and positions that have found the classical just war theory unacceptable. And it has connoted for some of its critics at times a sense of selfish opting out of the defence of others, of society and of civilisation. For its supporters it has been for some a clear demand of the gospel; for others, a demand of humanity itself, whether in a believer like Lactantius or an unbeliever like Bertrand Russell; for others, still the most effective response to the evils of war and violence; the only option left in face of possible total self-destruction; the best political strategy in a given situation or in a more selective sense the only way to react to a particular unjust war. Many of these positions are clearly related to the just war position. Some are based on the assessment of a particular war or all contemporary warfare as disallowed under the criteria of just cause (e.g. Vietnam for the US), just means (e.g. nuclear warfare or indiscriminate terrorism), or last resort (IRA in Ireland, PLO in the Middle East). These could be interpreted as particular applications of the just war theory. What is of more interest to this discussion is the recognition that rather than simply two polar positions of 'just war' and 'pacifism' there is a whole spectrum of positions between those two poles.

This may be further illuminated by recognising that the just war theorists never intended to make it easy to justify war, much less to glorify it. They found themselves, after Constantine for example, in the position of having to deal with actual warfare and consider the defence of the neighbour by the Empire. Their new-found responsibility led them to take a rather different line from that of their 'pacifist' predecessors who were 'without' the law of the Empire and certainly accepted no responsibility for its defence. The basis of their new justification of war was also love of neighbour which, in the context of attack on him, demanded that one come to his defence. Defending the neighbour out of love forms the heart of the theological justification of war. Because the aggressor is also to be loved, the various restraining conditions were worked out over the centuries. How far the love of neighbour and of enemy combined to moderate war may well be doubted. The exceptional cases of the Crusades, which many people would not include within their acceptance of the 'just war' tradition, show how dangerous such acceptance can be. Here are the frightening words of St Bernard of Clairvaux:

> The knights of Christ fight safely the battles of their Lord, in no wise fearing either sin from slaying enemies or the danger of their own destruction. Since indeed death for Christ must be either endured or dealt out to others, it invoketh no sin and indeed meriteth abundant glory. Indeed in the one case there is gain for Christ, in the other Christ is gained — Christ, who surely and willingly accepteth an enemy's death as retribution, and more willingly offereth Himself to the knight for consolation. A soldier of Christ, I say, slayeth with more honour for himself, and dieth with more merit. When he dieth himself is benefited; when he slayeth, he benefiteth Christ. For not without cause he beareth the sword. He is the minister of God for the punishment of those who do ill, but for the praise of those who do good. When he slayeth the doer of evil, he is not a manslayer, but — so I should say — a slayer of evil, and plainly an avenger of Christ against those who do wrong, and so he is accounted a defender of Christians . . . when the actual conflict hath commenced, they [the knights] at last put aside their former deliberateness, as if they should say: 'Do I not hate them, O Lord, who hate thee . . . and am not I at war with those who are hostile to thee?'[4]

While it may be fairly claimed that the Holy War or Crusade transcends the realities and arguments proper to the just war tradition, the difference is more one of degree than any absolute distinction or separation. This is confirmed by the religious wars of the sixteenth and seventeenth century. And the twentieth-century attitude to war as already exemplified in an episcopal sermon and as bloodily realised in the wars we have known, developed much of the crusading mentality. Eisenhower's 'Crusade in Europe' was succeeded or accompanied by crusades of East and West in Europe, Asia, Africa and Latin America. These ideological crusades of East and West were compounded by the nationalist, racist and even religious crusades with which they were connected. The holy war with its subordination of everything to the victory of its cause is not a remote horror of medieval Europe or darkest Africa. It is a living reality although seldom depicted in the terrifying colours which Frantz Fanon gives it in his essay 'Concerning Violence' in *The Wretched of the Earth.*

While still holding to the graduated range of attitudes and practices which have main focal points in the 'just war' position and the 'pacifist' position, it is clear how justified may be the fears of some pacifists that war is uncontrollable or at least usually uncontrolled. Yet they themselves have to face certain problems of force and violence on the domestic and broader social levels. Even if not all would be as forthright as Gandhi in denouncing cowardice as more dishonourable than fighting and in expecting his son to defend him should he be attacked, some of them acknowledge the need for protection of others, such as family, on the domestic level. Others concede the need for coercion to ensure peace and order within the society but feel the necessity to withdraw from such vocations themselves. Yet they depend on the existence of an ordered society.

Some of the inspiration and the practice of 'peace' groups derives from a rejection of the world or at least a judgment upon it that prevents them from taking a full part. The Christian community becomes an alternative society in a strong sense. This was at the base of the distinction between sect and church as developed particularly by Troeltsch. Yet in their different ways and admittedly to different degrees most Christian communities exhibit characteristics of both church and sect as far as acceptance of and integration into or rejection of and withdrawal from the broader society is concerned. In retaining this dual attitude and approach, Christian communities reflect the dual attitude to society or the world evident in the New Testament and exemplified in Christian history ever since. In so far as society or world is evil and sinful it is to be condemned and rejected. Christians are in it but not of it. In so far as it is God's work of creation, now subject to his redeeming and transforming grace and some sign and realisation of his inbreaking kingdom, it is to be celebrated and embraced. The mission of Christians to the discernment, preaching and realisation of the kingdom requires this dual attitude of rejecting and affirming the world in its ambiguity.

War and violence constitute a critical part of the ambiguity of the world, of its needs for redemption. Peace and righteousness or justice are to be characteristic features of the kingdom. The basic question for Christians is how do they overcome the violence and injustice which inhibit and contradict the kingdom but which are such pervasive features of the world in which they must live. The two traditions of the 'just war' and 'pacifism' have sought to address this question in their different ways. The temptation to 'crusade' and to 'total withdrawal' which have sometimes proved overwhelming for the one or the other tradition do not invalidate the basic truths they contain, the need in love to protect the neighbour from violence and injustice and the need to return love for hatred and hatred's expressions in violent attack. How Christians are to combine these two in this violent world has not as yet met with any universally accepted answer. The defenders of the just war marshal facts and arguments from contemporary situations. For the most part these defenders tend to concentrate on inter-state wars and Western Christians are sometimes particularly sensitive to the military threat of Communism. To be consistent they should apply their analysis to 'just revolution' within a state also. Those who reject the just war theory form a much less coherent group with much less uniform attitudes and approaches. The most coherent position, theoretically as well as practically effective, is that deriving from the work of Gandhi in India and Martin Luther King in the United States of America. In an interesting contrast they are mainly concerned with meeting violence within states whether from foreign or domestic 'tyrants'. Yet a great deal of attention has been given to replacing war at the interstate level, and to national defence also. Given the scope of this essay I will devote the rest of this chapter to an examination of the moral value of just revolution against a tyrannical government in comparison with non-violent approaches to radical political change. It will not, however, be possible to abstract from the larger

Christian context of the use or refusal of violence in war between states, 'necessary' coercion within states.

The earlier part of this chapter described with illustrations and some necessary qualifications the two basic traditions which Christians have defended on the use of violence for political purposes. The problem defines itself in so many areas today as one of whether the use of violence to protect or subvert the existing political order can be justified or not. Although, as I already indicated, this problem and the varying Christian responses to it are not entirely new, it is, for the purposes of this essay, useful to analyse and reflect on some of the more important dimensions of the use of violence in defence or for the overthrow of any particular political order.

Most political orders are established by violence and certainly use violence or the threat of violence to maintain themselves. Some people prefer to use the term 'force' in the context of upholding the established order, and may go on to distinguish this force as legitimate or morally justified, restricting the term violence to use of 'force' by those opposed to the established order. Some distinction between force and violence may have some advantages in distinguishing, say, the limited use of 'force' by police in protecting the citizens from the indiscriminate use of 'violence' by 'terrorists' attacking them. In the confused circumstances of so many current situations it is doubtful if the terms can be distinguished fairly and consistently. So it may be best to use only one of them as a 'neutral' term which derives its moral value from the circumstances in which it is used (analogous to 'just war' theory) or from the overall attitude to any use of force or violence (analogous to the pacifist tradition). Since, in the political arena, war, inter-state or intra-state, is commonly described as violence and the alternative as non-violence, I will use that term here. I am not unmindful, however, that force might be equally appropriate and in some circumstances might seem to some people to be even more appropriate.

I wish to distinguish three stages of the use of violence in the intra-state situation. I will offer some evaluation of these in the light of our previous theological discussion of state and politics and the Christian attitudes to different kinds of violence.

To fulfil its function in society and for the citizens, the state and its immediate servants will have to be prepared at least to restrain those who may not respect the lives and rights of people in society. Such restraint will inevitably do violence to the people identified as threatening others, by forcibly restricting their freedom of action. This kind of violence is justified in the moral tradition as part of the state's protective duty in relation to the citizens, but it is justified only in so far as it is necessary for such protection. The excesses beyond what is necessary for restraint, which may recur in particular incidents, may be understandable and excusable under provocation but are not morally justified in themselves. Obviously there is an enormous grey area between the use of violence in providing the necessary protection by restraint and the excesses that derive from 'zeal', misjudgment, fear, callousness or vindictiveness. To reduce the possibility of such excesses many police forces are forbidden to carry guns or lethal weapons. Yet even in such circumstances excesses frequently occur for the various reasons cited above, and people are actually killed. It is apparent that excesses by police in arresting and interrogating criminals, or by prison officers in treating those in their custody, have become an increasing problem even in the most stable of countries and those most respectful of human rights and the rule of law. Certain behaviour of British police and troops in Northern Ireland has been the subject of condemnatory reports and judgments, both under British auspices and, more clearly and importantly, under the auspices of independent and reputable bodies such as Amnesty International and the European Courts of Human Rights. Whatever excuses might be offered about Northern Ireland given its problems, and they do not seem to me adequate, the behaviour of police from Watts Co., Los Angeles, to Philadelphia to Southall, London, to take instances within the cherished Western way of respect for persons, their rights and the law, suggests real difficulties about the vision and discipline of police forces today. And of course to isolate the police forces, or even the particularly undisciplined or prejudiced elements among them, can be a form of escapism for the rest of us, providing us with our necessary scapegoats and letting us ignore the provocations and difficulties the police face.

The problem of police or prison-officer excess has to be dealt with fairly and effectively under the law but it raises deeper political questions about the nature of a particular society and its members' commitment to the welfare and development of all. The shadow side of any society is its criminal activity and society's response to that activity in its police courts and prisons reveals a good deal about the political well-being and priorities of that society. Even the violence of restraint, essential as it may appear in an ambiguous world to the survival and well-being of all people in society, may easily in excess become a counter-force to the well-being of certain people. It continually raises questions about the observance of law and of rights as well as about protection procedures and the deeper needs of society which must be met by a process of continuing reform. The most traditionally respected exercise of violence raises questions about political change which we ignore at our peril.

Accepting, in common with the majority of Christians past and present, the need for the violence of restraint in society, one is operating with criteria similar to those of the just war. The violence must be in the just cause of protecting the citizenry, the means used must be directed to and limited by the restraint necessary for the cause, the use should be duly authorised. To reject such exercise of violence means to adopt a very strong pacifist position and creates obvious difficulties in practice. It may also create difficulties in the Christian theory of love of neighbour if no violent and restraining intervention is allowed to protect the neighbour or even if one simply surrenders to the evil of the aggressor and does not attempt to protect him from the worst consequences of his aggression, his victim's death. The significance of such an extreme pacifist voice could be to get us away from much of the violence of restraint that is practised, which easily becomes excessive and in its excesses may be ineffectual. This voice summons us to seek more creative and imaginative ways of protection than the too readily and eagerly employed gun or truncheon with all their bloody consequences. It summons us further to the conversion of hearts and structures in political and personal reform which so much crime, petty and grave, unconsciously demands.

The tension between the 'realism', to use the Niebuhrean term, which most Christians accept as necessary and justified, and a 'pacifism' which would question even the limited violence of police-protection, is valuable politically as well as intellectually. Intellectually it challenges defenders of each tradition to reconsider its principles, their basis and their application, so that routine acceptance and flabby justification are never tolerated. Politically the tension between the two demands a careful analysis of the situations to which they are applied, whether in violent crime, protest, riot, or prison custody, as well as a continuous monitoring of the manner in which they are applied. Only such effects of the tension will prevent violent restraint from excess, challenging it to more creative alternatives and ensuring that the 'pacifists' accept responsibility for loving protection of neighbour.

What has been said here about protecting the members of society by state agencies, the justification of force or violence in that protecting and the possibility/reality of excesses, has assumed a certain basic moral legitimisation of the particular state and its activities. It has assumed therefore that excesses, however frequent, are opposed to state policy and subject to sanction themselves. It has assumed that the police and other protective agencies use their power only against those who attack the persons and rights of others and that any violation of this will be subject to state sanction under the law.

These assumptions are clearly not universally justified. Indeed it would be hard to find any state in which excesses did not occur and some class or racial or religious or even geographical bias was not at work in operating violence against alleged criminals. Yet there are many countries in which society can respond effectively to excess or bias either through state law and its officers or through other agencies such as the political opposition or the press or voluntary organisations or with various civil rights commitments. The church has its role in discerning and protesting against these failures. In these countries reform is continally possible as well as continually necessary, although it seldom occurs as quickly or as extensively as justice for the victims requires. In these countries, too, the 'pacifist' tradition may play a very important role in its sensitivity to the excessive or biased use of violence by the state and in the imaginative devising of means to protect and counter such violence. Its long-term role is to reduce if not remove what some citizens perceive as the necessity for state violence, exposing its users, as it does, to obvious temptations.

The violence of the state in its excess and bias is an insitutional violence that is certainly unjustified but may still be overcome in the conditions posited. There are many countries where the violence of the institution is reaching a new level and by that very fact tends to exclude the usual agencies of reform, from political opposition parties to free press to voluntary protest and reform groups. On occasion the church may be the only agency in society with the resources, freedom and prestige to protest against the violence and promote reform. And it too may be inhibited by state agencies or narrow self-interest.

The kind of situation in mind here ranges from dictatorship of the party in many communist countries to military dictatorships in a host of countries (from Latin America to Pakistan) to total control by a particular religious or racial group such as we have known in Southern Africa. These do not constitute a homogeneous political group and would be horrified to find themselves categorised together in this fashion. Yet for our purposes they have more in common than they realise. In excluding particular groups or whole peoples from participation in government, from a fair share in the goods and facilities of the society and equal freedom under the law, they are dissolving or very narrowly restricting that space between state and society within which human freedoms, differences and development can have effective play. What

is more relevant to the discussion of the violence they prac-
tise, the state-agencies such as the police act in a highly discriminatory way against the excluded or deprived groups.
This discrimination breeds excess because of the vulnerability
of the groups, who have little or no defence in law or in practice. The exclusion and privation often involve the denial
of a fair share of the goods and facilities available in terms
of food, clothing, shelter, educational and job opportunity
so that the victims are injured if not destroyed in their personal health and well-being. Such destruction of persons
and frequently of their meagre property by deliberate policy
of the state fully merits the title 'institutional violence'.
Taken together with the excesses and bias with which such
a policy is, indeed has to be, implemented, it provides
a fairly complete picture of the kind of violence that is abroad
in the world and frequently justified in the name of socialist
justice or law and order or Western civilisation or even
Christianity.

This is the kind of situation in which the question of
violent revolution can become acute. It is assumed that the
state's policy and its pursuit of violence, both structural
and actual, as outlined above, is exclusive, persistent and,
as far as history shows, closed to the kind of radical political
change that would liberate, integrate and protect the excluded,
the oppressed and the deprived. The basic injustice of the
situation is clear and enormous, and demands profound and
urgent righting. Who is to achieve that righting and how?

The first responsibility for righting the situation rests with
those who have power and are abusing it. Efforts can and
should be directed to persuading them to change the situation by people within the situation who have the freedom
or prestige or are at least conscious of the need. Given the
conditions of unyielding oppression it is difficult to demand
morally of people who may have already tried in vain and are
at any rate open to the retribution of the system and its
exploiters that they undertake this task of seeking to persuade. It is more difficult to excuse the Christian community
for refusing to address and challenge the people with power
even at the risk of serious loss to themselves as individuals

or to their institutional interests, whether in property or freedom of activity. To accept or appear to accept such institutional violence for the sake of the church's mission is self-defeating because it contradicts that mission's essential relationship to love of neighbour and promotion of the kingdom. How the refusal to accept such violence and how the further obligations of the church are best carried out in a particular situation will depend on the situation itself and the courage and sensitivity of Christians in discerning and responding to it.

Moral obligations to seek to persuade the political leaders to reform the situation also apply to people outside the situation who may have particular connections with the state in question — e.g. Britain with Rhodesia, USA in the past with Nicaragua — and who have some leverage, political or economic, in the situation. This is true, in varying degrees, of individual states and international political groupings from the United Nations to the European Economic Community. Failure to comply or, more reprehensibly, violation of agreed measures of at least partially effective pressure and persuasion such as economic sanctions or sports boycotts, can be a serious breach of duty and solidarity. It can leave the victims of such power-play helpless for generations or goad them into the violent reaction which they eventually consider to be their only hope of change. Even if the attempts to establish a just international order and so to influence the internal disorder of certain states, display some of the characteristics of the task of Sisyphus, they also demand the persistent heroism which Camus suggests in his version of the myth. They carry, too, a hope or meaning that may be long denied and never fully realised. Such hope or meaning need not be evasions in the Camus sense, but spurs to great heroism and more persistent efforts.

The ineffectiveness of much outside advice and help is usually evident to the oppressed. When it does not derive simply from self-interest (making this state safe for our multinationals or our goods or our oil-resources), it is frequently seen as dangerous to self-interest. The lesson of Vietnam may be more sophisticated than that usually presented as the folly of interfering directly in another state or of committing troops on the ground. That simple lesson, which Britain may have learned earlier than the US, suffices to keep individual states bystanders even in the face of such clear responsibility as Britain had after UDI in Rhodesia. The intervention of the United Nations is largely restricted by the political interests and fears of individual members. So while a Tanzania may find the right occasion and enjoy the moral opportunity to depose an Amin, the exploited in a particular state must to a great extent rely on themselves.

Is that self-reliance in resisting oppression and pursuing radical change to take a violent or non-violent form? In many situations, due to the sheer weight of the oppression it is impossible or too soon to speak of exercising either option effectively. The sort of underground education and solidarity which might develop among the oppressed is usually threatened by secret police, informers and security measures. Here it may be for the churches to give a lead, even at great cost to themselves.

With consolidation and leadership and perhaps a let-up for various reasons in the regime's control of the situation, people may turn to a more open struggle, armed or unarmed. In fact in most situations the struggle takes both armed and unarmed forms. The questions to be decided, however, are: how far is the armed struggle necessary and justified? How far can it be replaced by an unarmed struggle that will be equally — and perhaps more — effective?

It is possible for 'just war' defenders to apply the criteria developed in that tradition concerning just cause, last resort, fair means and due proportion about the evils entailed by war as opposed to current evils. This last connects with 'the hope of success' criterion frequently invoked in these cases. The question of authority revolves around the loss of legitimacy by the oppressive government and the interpretative right of the opposition leaders to speak for the oppressed.

Opponents of the 'just war' theory cannot of course accept this kind of analysis and its application to a particular situation. They could and should lead the way in devising alternative strategies. These should include educational or consciousness-raising programmes about the dignity and rights of the oppressed as well as collaborative enterprises which reveal and respect their dignity and help them meet their more basic needs and rights in food, health-care, educational development, work and community, church and organisation. How to do all this will, in many instances, tax the imagination and ingenuity, the courage and persistence of the leaders. But their genuine commitment to non-violent ways of human protection and caring and political change demands of them as much.

The role for Christians and particularly church leaders in such work is clear and urgent. However one feels about the justice of revolution in theory, it has enormously evil consequences in practice and can have very destructive after-effects e.g. lack of reconciliation within a country and the reinforcing of the tradition that violence pays in promoting or subverting the new regime. To escape from that historical cycle is not easy. But the non-violent alternative in promoting necessary political change and preserving justice and peace can, if pursued effectively, reduce the current evil and act as a preventive for the future. So for people who may consider just revolution theoretically or actually defensible, alternatives may still be possible and fruitful. To make them fruitful demands the commitment, education and training which we automatically expect of armed revolutionaries. It demands strategy, tactics and skills which are not acquired by instinct or good will but are the result of training and consultation and learning by experience. It involves leadership and organisation, which will not come about haphazardly. Such a movement has the double task of caring for and educating the deprived themselves and on appropriate occasions verifying, protesting and then resisting the oppressive actions of the powerful.

The identification with the oppressed by sharing their world of oppression enables Christians to demonstrate their love of neighbour and commitment to justice. Their continuous pursuit of this, drawing on biblical and Christian traditions as well as the more recent thoughts and experiences of Gandhi and Martin Luther King, will be directed first of all to liberating the oppressed. However, in achieving the liberation in this way and dissolving the oppressive power-relationships, a contribution is also made to the liberation of the oppressors enslaved by their power and property. A situation is created in which fuller emancipation may occur and genuine reconciliation becomes a possibility. This would be excluded by simply reversing the power structure and replacing the old oppressors by new, a danger in the aftermath of so many violent struggles. At least it would establish a new tradition of political change and the overcoming of oppression for that state and perhaps others.

In many instances, therefore, the Christian role is to denounce, oppose and seek to overcome the oppression. In the world today this role must be taken further than rejection of violence on both sides to providing leadership in devising effective strategies for radical change which involve the least violence and provide the deepest and most concrete type of structural and personal emancipation, conversion and reconcilation.

4.

Prayer and Politics

The conflict within the Christian believer, and within the church between the believer's dependence on God and his responsibility as a human being, is no fresh discovery to be attributed to the coming of age of mankind, the rapid progress of secularisation or, as is the theme of this book, the concern of Church and techology with social and political justice.[1] In both the Old and New Testaments the dialectic between saying 'Lord' and behaving as neighbour has to be continually invoked if the faith that effectively loves is not to collapse into empty ritual or arrogant assumption of divine status. The dialectic is no less necessary today. For the comfortable of the first world the ritual reassurance of 'Lord, Lord,' is insidiously seductive. For the oppressed of the third world the temptation to reject the God of Jesus Christ as the totem of the oppressors and to take the world into their own hands may prove irresistible. For the one, prayers for peace (really the 'no-peace' of Jeremiah) become a substitute for action; for the other the futility of prayer has long been exposed, the point is not to pray about their condition but to change it. Mary and Martha comparisons do not fit very easily into the drawing-rooms of the affluent or the mud huts of the poor, into the executive suites of the powerful or the torture centres or prisons for the powerless. Yet if the dialectic between prayer and action collapses, the emptiness and frustration of oppressor and oppressed will be further increased. One of the strongest impressions of my recent visits to Rhodesia and of my conversations with people on the different sides of the racial and political divides

79

was the need to redefine the relationship between prayer and politics and develop some kind of spirituality of liberation for all the enslaved, powerful and powerless. The simplistic criticisms of church involvement in 'liberation' by Dr Edward Norman, recent Reith lecturer on BBC, among others, has reinforced my sense of the urgency of this task.

Prayer and Liberation

The old-fashioned catechism description of prayer as raising the mind and heart to God retains its validity and provides a convenient starting-point. In its way it underlines what is in the recent jargon called the transcendent openness of humankind. As emphasised earlier, persons and communities, however conditioned by historical circumstances, are not confined by them or to them. They have this openness to what is beyond the present situation of achievement or failure. They are open and receptive to the transcendent — in Christian terms, God, Creator and Redeemer. In prayer individually and communally Christians (and other religious people) act on behalf of the human community and of creation in enabling them to respond to and receive the personal God who is their source and destiny. By a paradoxical act of condescension the Creator and Lord of all awaits and depends on this receptivity of humankind at prayer. The receptive ability itself is of course God's gift and so is the energy and will by which it is exercised. Yet he stands at the door and knocks. He enters by invitation only. The most remarkable feature of prayer is not what it does for man but what it does 'for' God. It allows him to enter his own world most intimately and properly by entering the minds and hearts of human beings. The first liberating effect of human prayer is its liberation of God, permitting him to be himself in the intimacy of human hearts. Letting the Creator be himself in his own world is the critical achievement of genuine prayer, personal and communal, private and liturgical, vocal, silent, contemplative and mystical. By conferring on God the freedom of the whole city of mankind, the Christian churches and other religious groups at prayer fulfil their primary mission to God and to mankind.

But the God of Jesus Christ is not the God of individuals or of human hearts and minds only. He is the God of the whole world, of history, of society, of all men in the totality of their personal and social relationships. His coming in prayer into hearts and minds must be extended into communities, relationships and structures if he is to enjoy his full and proper freedom in his own world. God's liberation through prayer will remain shackled and confined if it does not move through and become embodied in the full range of human structures, attitudes and activities. To liberate God by prayer and to refuse him free range in familial, social, political and economic life is to insult him and to contradict oneself. The freedom of God to be himself in the world at large is not achieved by ecclesiastical control but by the coming of the kingdom in society in a way already discussed in chapter two, and to be further discussed below. Here the concern is clear that the primary role of prayer in liberating God in his own world demands accompanying and appropriate liberating activity in society.

The liberation of God is the other side of the history of human salvation. Human sin and failure has prevented God from being himself properly and fully in his world. His continued initiatives in eliciting human cooperation in achieving this liberation which reached a climax in Jesus Christ, finally ensured human ability and willingness to let God be himself. Not only was God liberated in this way but by becoming himself for mankind, he achieved his full identity in the world as Father, Son and Holy Spirit. The idols of the past were shattered. Fresh idols arise and have to be shattered so that God's self-identification which he promised to Moses and the people of Israel ('I will be who I will be') may be constantly realised. And the obscurities and veils of the past were at least removed to the point where the internal liberation of God and his self-identification in history as Father, Son and Holy Spirit could be achieved. Faith as prayer and faith as social commitment are not only ways of recognising this identity, transcendent yet historical, but provide the human context in which God can express himself as who he really is in his unity and trinity. Politics no less than prayer contribute to God attaining his own identity in the ambiguous history of mankind.

The particular attainment of that divine identity in human history involves simultaneously the challenge to the attainment of human identity in Jesus Christ as sons and daughters of the Father, brothers and sisters of one another. To affirm one's identity by saying 'Father' underpins human subjectivity, ability to respond out of oneself in history to the ultimate subject with whom one's destiny rests. Achieving human identity, granted at this level in Jesus Christ, is possible only in and through history, although it is never complete in history. The way of identification is the way of becoming subject in history and so the way of salvation. It is not an individual way. The 'Father' is 'Our Father' not my father. The sons and daughters of 'Our Father' can attain their identity and subjectivity and salvation only as brothers and sisters. Identity, like subjectivity and liberation, is a social reality, challenging the depersonalising structures and relationships of history, calling for the restoration of those people absent from history, the naming of those with no name in the street or the bush or the servants' quarters.

The liberating of God into human history and the attainment of his own identity there cohere also with the understanding of the kingdom which Jesus preached and inaugurated and for whose coming we pray. The liberated presence of God as himself is his presence in loving, saving power and kingly rule. That power and rule may not be restricted to the minds and hearts of believers but have far-reaching implications for the whole of society as we have seen. The simplest and most direct understanding of the relationship between prayer and social and political activity is the direct concern of both activities for the coming of the kingdom and its values. To neglect either is to falsify the basic and unified Christian commitment.

Social and Political Activity as Prayer

From prayer to social and political activity as expression of brotherhood, recognition of Jesus in the deprived, love of the marginalised neighbour and service of the coming kingdom seems in many ways a necessary and relatively clear step for Christians to take. The step from social and political activity to prayer seems less obvious, and to many activists scarcely necessary. Yet for Christians and others that step has in different ways immense significance.

Christians can make the connection between prayer and politics in their heads and hearts at their prayer. Do they make such connection at their politics? If they do not and cannot, must the two lives exist side by side, acknowledged by faith (of a rarefied kind) to be at one but without any felt relationship? How long will the interaction survive without a more deeply rooted and experienced connection? The most direct and helpful way into this problem may be to examine the dynamics of discerning and caring for others personally and structurally which politics involves. The focus of one's attention, recognition, and loving care and activity is other human beings, individually and in groups. Such attention and recognition as is focused on the other take one beyond the self to the world of the other. The further care and response, often over time and through structures, express the same dynamic reaching out beyond the self to the other. But the other remains beyond one's grasp, a centre of its own, given to one as gift but still an irreducible centre of recognising, caring and acting in its own right. One reaches such others at their gracious invitation. They finally elude and challenge one with their unconditional demand for recognition and respect as unique, inviolable and creative beings. Their irreducibility, inviolability and creativity reveal at once the richness and opacity of the others. (And so of the self, which is also a human other calling for the same recognition and respect in return.) The others become not only focuses of concern but subjects of respect and awe in the recognition of individual and communal value and worthship. They form subjects of worship, finally mysterious in their irreducible value and worth.

The qualities which characterise this recognition of the others as irreducible gift and value are the qualities of thanksgiving and humility and respect and awe. They are the qualities of prayer and in Christian faith terms properly so. For in human persons, the penultimate others, one encounters the ultimate and divine other, source of their irreducible human otherness, of their particular identity as subjects in history and of their destiny as sons and daughters of the Father. The inherent dynamism and characteristic qualities of social and political commitment and service where it is really focused on human beings, whether directly and personally or indirectly through complex structures, carry that commitment and service on to the source of human value and otherness, the transcendent God. For believers social and political activity are transcended in prayer. Prayer in turn is nourished and developed by recognising and feeling the dynamism at work in all of human life and by experiencing the living qualities of thanksgiving and humility, respect and awe, repentance and reconciliation which service demands and which are also the stuff of prayer. To restore to prayer the vitality it may have lost in religious formulas, one should invoke and relate the true qualities of the work of social and political liberation. If that service and liberation are to reach beyond the closer horizons of any particular history and society they must be followed through and transcended in prayer.

The risks are obvious and need little elaboration. Instead of reaching for the transcendent Other in response to the human other one may remain content, closed, enslaved in a limited and finally frustrated humanism. One may plunge through the penultimate others to the ultimate, using people as stepping stones to Christ or God and so in fact finally miss God as one steps over and ignores these 'least ones'. Yet the renewal of prayer through understanding and following through the thrust of service to others forms a critical challenge and a real possibility in our time.

Suffering and Liberation

The classical difficulties which human suffering pose for belief in an all-powerful and all-loving God yield to no easy solutions. The appeal to resignation in view of the reward of the next world, when not simply the self-serving counsel of the comfortable, remains vulnerable to the Marxist criticism of using religion as an opiate to keep the oppressed docile. With the fuller understanding of Christian faith as demanding justice, of the Church as committed to promoting kingdom values and of prayer as the transcendent dimension of political activity in allowing God to be himself in his own world, some deeper reflection on the Christian meaning and reaction to suffering is required. The concern here is with the suffering of those exploited and oppressed by political structures and of those (who are at least in some places some of the same people) caught in the violent interaction of rebellion and repression.

The suffering of the oppressed is by definition unjust. Its further Christian significance is not injustice, but blasphemy, the defacing of the image of God in his people, the restriction of his liberty to be himself in his world. The moral and Christian response called for is to overcome the oppression as humanly and quickly as possible. This is as much for the sake of the oppressors as of the oppressed. The oppressors must be restrained if they are to be released from their blasphemy, or at least given the opportunity to discover anew the God of Jesus Christ, the God of all suffering servants.

In such a situation a Christian community will not just pity the oppressed and seek to relieve their sufferings in some paternalistic and patronising way. Its commitment to overcome those sufferings will be modelled on the person and activity of Jesus as he sought to feed the hungry, set the captives free, heal the sick and even restore the dead to life. It will be spontaneous, practical and persevering like that of Jesus himself or his Samaritan type-figure. The church's expression of that commitment will achieve solidarity with the suffering by sharing their conditions and their cause. Such solidariaty is not easy to attain. Not every member of the church will attain it to the same degree. But unless the church as a whole affirms that solidarity and seeks to attain it in varying degrees and unless some representative groups and individuals truly share the worst conditions of the suffering, supported by the rest of the church, the church's stance will not be credible or effective.

This solidarity expresses our human brotherhood and sister-hood and our commitment to equal justice for all. For Christians that solidarity is one of brotherhood and sisterhood of Christ, daughterhood and sonship of the Father. The moral ties are deeper and more urgent than those of merely human brotherhood. And they are not just moral ties, deriving from our faith. An exercise of our faith, of our search for and discovery of God is involved. It was such excluded and rejected people that Jesus sought out in his mission. More significantly it was in becoming excluded, rejected and suffering unto death at the hands of the religious and political establishments that he liberated us to God and God to us. Christian solidarity with the suffering is closely connected with the search for God. For the struggle of the suffering the presence of God is, by the lesson of the Cross, to be more clearly and strongly discovered. The haunting story of his concentration camp experiences, by Elie Wiesel in *Night* (New York 1972), illustrates this very powerfully:

> The SS hung two Jewish men and a boy before the as-sembled inhabitants of the camp. The men died quickly but the death struggle of the boy lasted half an hour. As the boy, after a long time, was still in agony on the rope, I heard the man cry again, 'Where is God now?' And I heard a voice within me answer, 'Here he is — he is hanging on this gallows.'

Solidarity with the suffering is solidarity with Jesus, the original sacrament or effective sign of the saving presence of God. To ignore the suffering or play with caring for them, is to ignore that presence of God or trivialise it. It is to identify with the blasphemy of oppression. For it is, in the Hebrew prophetic tradition as well as in the Christian tradi-tion, impossible to belong to the oppressors of humankind and worship the one true God. To pretend to do so is indeed blasphemy.

The solidarity must not degenerate into the acceptance of suffering on behalf of the oppressed. Their conviction that God is with them may and should help them to endure what might otherwise be unendurable. But it is not simply a summons to submission but to salvation, to liberation for them, for their God and even for their oppressors. Protest against oppression (and its blasphemy) must, as Gustavo Guttierez points out, always accompany solidarity. Solidarity is in this fashion kept honest and honourable for the people who join the oppressed. The protest will seek to change the conditions, to overcome the oppression, to let true human fulfilment emerge, to release God who is captive also. The efforts for liberation, embodying respect for human dignity and God-given worth, enter into the true spirituality of the oppressed. But such efforts may be long in coming. They may frequently be inadequate. They may sometimes be distorted. The manner and the persistent pursuit of them will require further surrender and suffering in the disciplined loving that is born of faith in the liberating God of Jesus Christ, and hope and trust in his availability even to the mighty oppressors who must be cast down from their thrones and yet eventually integrated into the reconciling work of God in Jesus. Overcoming the oppression is a demand of Christian faith, finally forgiving and accepting the oppressors is no less a demand of Christian love. In pursuing that two-staged task, a Christian spirituality for political struggle will be born. One kind of suffering, that of the politically oppressed, will yield up its resurrection fruits.

PART II

From Rhodesia to Zimbabwe:
A Theological Reflection

5.

Conquest, Colony and Church

As I sit down to write, elections under the March 1978 Agreement have just been completed with a 64 per cent vote claimed for the African population and Bishop Muzorewa's party enjoying an overall majority of 51 seats out of 100. What Ian Smith proclaimed just three years ago — that never in a thousand years and certainly never in his lifetime would there be an African majority government — has been achieved with his cooperation and at least public approval. It might seem that the long agony of the Rhodesian people, black and white, was over; that Britain, the responsible colonial power, might rush to recognition followed by its western allies; that economic sanctions might be lifted and the new state take its place in the ordinary way in the international community. At any rate it might seem that the crisis which the churches have had to endure in trying to serve two peoples with strongly divergent and even murderously conflicting political goals might be at an end. Whatever the fate of the new government in the external political order, and it is by no means assured of acceptance, the internal struggle seems likely to continue and the role of the churches to be as difficult and dangerous in the near future as it has been in the recent past. To understand that past role and to prepare for the future it is necessary to recover some of the past to see how the political structure may have shaped the churches and the churches influenced the political structure.

This is not intended as a historical survey following the canons of historical work but as a theologian's selection and reflection, attempting to be as fair as possible while directed

91

towards theological and moral assessment. In accordance with my general purpose I will concentrate on the Catholic church but with at least background advertence to the difficulties and achievements of the other churches and such major figures as Arthur Shirley Cripps and Guy Clutton-Brock. In this chapter I will be endeavouring to understand how the Catholic church leadership by and large saw itself and its mission predominantly through European expatriate eyes. In the next chapter the angle of vision will be different.

Colonisation and the origins of the churches

Although, even before Rhodes's Pioneer Column reached Harare/Salisbury in 1890, there had been Christians missionaries in the territory subsequently known as Rhodesia,[1] Christian, including Catholic, missions really began in an organised fashion after that. Priests and sisters actually arrived with the Column and were naturally ministering to the colonisers at the beginning. This established for Catholic missionaries, as well as for other missionaries in colonial countries, a context of operation and a source of identification from which they found it very hard to escape in the minds of the colonists, the colonised and indeed in their own minds. Much of the subsequent division in the Catholic church which I found to be so acute in Zimbabwe/Rhodesia stemmed from the entanglements, the loyalties and the resentments created in this early colonial period.

Taking for granted its pastoral responsibility to the first settlers, the church inevitably understood the opening up of the land north of the Limpopo as an opportunity to preach the gospel to native peoples whom they regarded as simply pagan and who had been for geographic, climatic and political reasons largely inaccessible hitherto. The gospel to be preached was the Good News of Salvation in Jesus Christ which involved conversion from their pagan beliefs and practices and the gradual establishment of the Christian church. It was a basically religious mission and the missionaries considered themselves outside and above politics. How far this was or could ever be fully true would take us too far afield here.

To ignore particular political policies is frequently in practice to support if not endorse them. And the mental attitudes and life-style of many missionaries were reflections of those of the settlers. They accepted the colonisation process as a natural and inevitable result of the inherent superiority of the white race and civilisation and the need to develop the lands and resources of the native peoples, even for their own sake. And in this they saw a providential opportunity to bring the gospel to the Africans.

Their 'missionary purity' did not prevent them from accepting tracts of land from the Company, although they did, for the most part, try to use these not for personal gain after the fashion of the conventional settlers but as a basis for establishing and training African communities. In a way these mission lands revealed the ambiguity of their position from the beginning. To establish themselves and carry on their mission work they depended on the generosity of the colonial powers in sharing with them some of the spoils of conquest, a conquest coloured both by the fraud practised in the original agreement with King Lobengula and by the blood of so many killed in the rebellions of 1893 and 1896. Given the confusion of the times, the consciousness of white superiority in race and civilisation, the missionaries' dependence on white power for 'law and order' in face of the 'barbarians', and the opportunity for mission, it may be disappointing but not entirely surprising that those missionaries allowed their white settler friends to ignore the basic moral problems raised by occupation, conquest and exploitation, while they got on with their 'gospel' work.

During and after the wars of rebellion, they did exercise some moderating influence on the settler desire for revenge and need to teach these people a lesson. Such a moderating and mediating influence, however limited it really was, constituted one of their major contributions to the social development of Rhodesia as it is now came to be called. As interpreters of language, law and other settler demands, they tried at times to protect the Africans from the more unjust demands of individual settlers and their officials. In their own mission stations and in their direct contact with the Africans they displayed some of the personal kindness and care which their calling as Christian missionaries demanded. This calling took them further, over the years, into providing education and medical care, assisting in community development in various ways. It did not, however, lead them into confronting the government on what they considered to be political issues, issues that excluded the African people from a fair share in land, wealth, education, health care and political power, these benefits lying within the exclusive control of the tiny minority of white settlers.

The facts and figures of Rhodesian development-exploitation provide a fascinating but extended story. Indeed they provide two stories, almost as irreconcilable as black and white, the two perspectives and sources which determine them. The first settlement and the wars of rebellion have different heroes, differing accounts of victory and defeat. The gradual occupation of the fertile lands, the mineral resources, their development, the white management and the recruitment of black labour, the building of white cities and then, reluctantly and miserably, of black townships, disclose some of the major differences in the two stories of development on the one hand and exploitation on the other. Exclusion of blacks from white politics because they were seen as unready and irresponsible except for the few who were later admitted on criteria basically designed to keep them out, or the prohibition of black organised labour, or the regulation of land by the 1930 Land Act or of native agriculture by the 1951 Act, all had their white justifications and black rejections. The missionaries sometimes joined in the justifications, believing that the 1930 Land Act would afford some protection for black purchasers or that the 1951 Act was in the Africans' own interests. They were not so frequently heard in those years, at least not the Catholic ones, criticising the general policy and the particular laws and practices whereby the whites enjoyed all the power and privileges and the Africans were left with the crumbs. Such criticism as distinct from occasional praise would have been 'interfering in politics' and would have handicapped, in this view, the important religious, educational and other services which they were providing for the Africans. It was a dilemma with which the churches has to struggle for many decades.

Equality Before God

The gospel message which prevailed in the late nineteenth and early twentieth centuries was primarily a message of salvation or fulfilment in the next world. The morality for this world which it clearly presented was an individualist morality whereby the individual saved his soul by observing the commandments, which were seen, however, as demands to respond to individual others. The days of social morality and justice were still ahead.

The church's catastrophic loss of the working class in Europe in the aftermath of the Industrial Revolution, and the beginnings of a response which led to Leo XIII's encyclical *Rerum Novarum,* could not be expected to equip missionaries in Southern Africa quickly or adequately to face a whole new set of social problems there, combining the most intractable features of economic power and racial superiority. Their gospel message was much simpler than that. It did not seek to cope with pass laws or derisory wages or prohibition of unions. Yet it had some sense of the value and dignity of every person. It could hardly claim to preach the gospel at all and ignore that. Such gospel equality undoubtedly influenced individual missionaries and people close to them in their work. But it lacked real social and political bite. This is admirably illustrated in the first pastoral letter issued by Archbishop Aston Chichester, Rhodesia's first Catholic bishop. While declaring his intention of remaining aloof from politics he affirmed in the name of church that 'in the presence of God every living soul is equal' (1931).[2]

In many ways this underlines the weakness of the church. Yet it would be mistaken to dismiss this remark in cynical fashion. First of all the gospel tradition to which Archbishop Chichester and all of us are heirs must always start from this basic premise. The love which God has for each of us, the love which impelled him to send his only Son, gives a depth and significance to our dignity and equality which no privation or exploitation can destroy. In the midst of the worst of oppression to have this sense of one's dignity is a reassurance and consolation which may not be easily taken away. It also reminds us that we have no lasting city here and that our dignity and equality will finally receive a recognition that no earthly power and wealth could match. For men of Archbishop Chichester's time and background this was at the heart of the gospel; it was what they really came to offer the people, not any political kingdom. They further believed that if all Christians (in this case white Christians) took this gospel seriously, then the deprivation and oppression would in fact be removed. However, they did not see it as their task to enter actively into that removal process where it involved political action. They did not even seem to consider it their business to analyse and criticise morally the structures or legislation which embodied the privations of which they could hardly have been unaware. The equality and the dignity which concerned them were theological and perhaps philosophical. They did not translate into legal, social or economic realities. Theyd did not involve concrete moral denunciation and demand in these areas. Practical works of charity on a private basis in schools and clinics were the most forceful expression of this theology of equality. The gospel of justice was yet to be born.

The Gospel of Justice

The narrow interpretation of the gospel, which formed the regular teaching and thinking of the missionaries through so much of the Catholic world at this time, was open to the old objection canonised by Marx that religion was being used to keep the people quiet, to get them to accept intolerable conditions of living and working here and now, on promise of fulfilment hereafter. No doubt some colonial masters were hoping to use the missionaries in this way. It is an aspiration and a practice as old as politics and religion. Given their European background, sense of superiority and fears for the breakdown of law and order, some missionaries, perhaps most, were influenced by the desire to assist in controlling and gradually assimilating the more educated Africans into the white system. From their point of view this would be an advancement for the Africans and provide continuity and order in a continent where, by the 1950s, discontinuity and disorder were beginning to manifest themselves, with inevitable loss to religion and civilisation. In this atmosphere the establishment of the Federation of Central Africa, comprising Southern Rhodesia as it was then called, Northern Rhodesia (now Zambia) and Nyasaland (now Malawi), seemed a political step forward particularly as it emphasised partnership between the races. The church could now, as it were, get a handle on the racial problem and found a concrete expression for its theology of equality in the policy of multiracialism. As an ideal it seemed eminently evangelical. However the actual reactions of the proposed partners might have given reason for doubt about its ultimate fate. For Sir Godfrey Huggins (later Lord Malvern), first Prime Minister of the Federation, the partnership was like that of the rider and the horse. The horse was clearly black. The further developments of the Federation with the centre of power, activity and wealth remaining in Salisbury, and Southern Rhodesia always regarded as the more racist of the three countries, served to increase the African opposition which had been strong from the beginning but effectively ignored. And it was the burgeoning time of African nationalism throughout the continent. Sharing the colonial administration and wealth was no longer the goal. Majority vote and self-rule were concrete demands. Rhodesia for all its historical peculiarities could be no exception and the first genuine nationalist party was founded in 1957 with Joshua Nkomo as Chairman.

The church's hopes for multiracialism may have made it rather more politically conscious. At any rate by now it was dominated by blacks and whites who had not the same close and confusing ties with the colonial administration. Many of its missionaries were recent, not of British background and working far from the inevitably collusive atmosphere of Salisbury. They were predominantly men in the bush and in close daily contact with Africans. Whatever may have been the conjunction of forces, a growing awareness of the injustices to which the Africans were subject began to find fresher and stronger expression. Equality before God or even the ideal of a multi-racial society must now yield to the urgent need to denounce publicly the clear social injustices under which the Africans suffered. Social justice was a demand of the gospel and obligatory teaching for the church. The man who made the breakthrough for the Catholic church was Bishop Donal Lamont of Umtali with his pastoral letter *A Purchased People* in 1959.[3] Still maintaining that he was not interfering in politics, he felt bound as a bishop to announce to his people the social implications of the gospel as he had received them through the medium of Catholic social teaching. The seed sown by Leo XIII and nurtured by Pius XI and Pius XII bore new and healthy fruit in the heartland of Southern Africa. Equality before God and reward in the next life had suddenly taken human and historical shape in the words of Rhodesia's most influential white churchman for twenty years to come. The church could no longer be depended on to keep the 'natives' quiet. Servicing the colonial structure was no longer an accusation that could easily be made.

The sequence of political events in the early sixties, through the negotiations leading to the 1961 Constitution, the rise of the Rhodesian Front, the coming to power of Ian Smith and the eventual Declaration of Independence in 1965, had its complex African counterpart. Multiracialism seemed dead on both sides. Any prospect of compromise by the whites was gradually extinguished. The extremism of the Rhodesian Front commanded the support of the vast majority of the whites. The blacks too, after the failure of the 1961 negotiations and the banning and arrest of many of their leaders and parties, were moving into a position of 'majority rule now' and there was the feeling that it might have to be won by force of arms. The Catholic church became increasingly vocal, at least at the episcopal level and tried to combine a firm rejection of the injustices with an appeal for negotiated agreement. By 1965 it was clearly opposed to the injustices suffered by the Africans at the hands of the now illegal regime. However, it tried to maintain its stance of being outside politics and of merely discharging its moral duty in denouncing the worst excesses of the regime.

Political Confrontation

The church's distance from direct involvement in politics was considerably reduced, if not actually eliminated, by the Constitution and Land Tenure Act introduced by the Rhodesian Front government in 1969.[4] The Constitution made explicit what had been clear practice for some time: that the people of Rhodesia who were consulted and protected were simply the whites. These were further reduced in governmental thinking to supporters of the RF. These supporters had their thinking done for them by ruling members who may not even have included the whole cabinet. Bishop Lamont's remark that Rhodesia was a state without a nation was in fact an understatement. Not only were the black people, who might have constituted 95 per cent of the nation or total society, excluded from any effective part in power; so too were the white critics and opponents of the regime. Not to support RF and 'good ole Smithy' was equivalent to treason. The collapse of any distinction between society and state, a distinction which, as the earlier part of this book maintains, is vital to protecting human rights, had been long in the making but seemed now formally accomplished. Such a state could not of course make a real exception for religious liberty, even on such a strictly religious issue as worship.

The Land Act, which gave a further refinement to the earlier exploitative divisions, now forbade the occupation of white land by blacks or of black lands by whites without the express permission of the relevant minister of state. Such occupation was understood to mean attendance at schools, hospitals and even churches. Given the church involvement in all of these institutions and given above all the critical issue of having white priests and people attend mass on black land or black priests and people attend mass on white land, there did not appear to be any way in which the church could surrender to a minister of state the right to decide who would celebrate or attend masses in which churches.

The confrontation which now developed no longer involved denunciation of injustice at some distance but a political power struggle of the church for basic freedom to operate its minimal and central service. From preaching equality before God as a message of the gospel to increasingly pointed moral denunciation while claiming to remain outside politics, the church as an institution now found itself facing the state as an institution on what was to it a matter of life and death: was it to be allowed to act as truly church or was it to be just another administrative department of the one-party — almost one-man — state which had long abandoned the way of limited government with the consent of the governed and respect for their human rights? The unsatisfactory practical resolution of this confrontation and the inevitable loss of face to the church did allow the church to carry on much of its institutional activity, and the era of eye-ball to eye-ball confrontation between bishops and ministers of state had passed with some useful lessons for both.

These events were overshadowed by the Home-Smith Agreement between Britain and Rhodesia in 1971 and its unexpected and overwhelming rejection by the Africans under the leadership of Bishop Muzorewa. The black nation had found its voice again and the way was open for a restoration of black leadership and influence in creating a society based on justice and a state based on the will of all the people. Smith and the RF were as adamant as ever. The church maintained its stance of exposing and denouncing injustice. But the thoughts of the blacks were no longer of external negotiations through Britain and the United Nations, or of internal negotiations with the evidently intransigent and racist RF. The intermittent violence which had surfaced during the sixties entered upon a new and, as it transpired, continuing stage in December 1978. The problems which this created for a church seriously engaged in the condemnation of the pervasive injustice and rejection which the African people had endured for so long and which the RF regime refused to regard as suitable matters for negotiation, properly belong to the next chapter. It is worth mentioning at this stage that if a church by its denunciations helps to awaken a people to their oppression, it must ask itself serious questions about what means are available to overcome the oppression. When the violence has started it is usually too late to say 'But that is not what we meant at all.'

A New Way of Church Leadership in Society

Despite the set-back which the church authorities appeared to have suffered over the Land Act in acquiescing in the government's compromise solution that the church would be deemed for the present to have sought and received permission to have racial mixing in church and other church institutions (within very narrow limits — for example, in schools), the church did not simply abandon its earlier moral responsibility. In some respects the era for that type of confrontation may have passed. At any rate the formation, in accordance with the demands of the Second Vatican Council, of a local Commission for Justice and Peace involving laity and clerics, enabled the church to develop a new way of providing effective and concrete moral leadership of a kind that scarcely any country had developed before. The Commission for Justice and Peace was of course, as originally intended, a pooling of church resources for the further education of people in the doctrine and practice of these basic dimensions of the gospel as they now had come to be seen. However, the Salisbury-based Commission, under its episcopal presidents and with its committed lay and clerical, black and white staff, was not content to purvey papal teaching or deplore the latest atrocity in the war. It took its task far more seriously and despite risks to its members and their families culminating in the arrest, imprisonment and explusion of many, proved to be the most informed and effective critic of the institutionalised injustice and violence on which Rhodesia was built and maintained. Its careful collection of evidence and its publication of this with the assistance of the Catholic Institute of International Relations in London, have been of enormous value in explaining to the world and to those Rhodesians willing to listen what has really been going on. In some of this work it was anticipated by *Moto,* a newspaper founded by the church in the 1960s but subsequently banned by the Smith regime.

These two institutions indicate how in one particular situation the church's commitment to justice and its consequent need to criticise and oppose the established injustice may be attempted without turning the church into an alternative political party or state. My theological understanding of this compels me to distinguish state and society. The denial of this distinction by Rhodesia made things very difficult but on the political side the triumph over the Smith-Home arrangement and on the church side the activities of the Commission or of *Moto* upheld the distinction in spite of all kinds of harassment. The church's mission seems to me to be for, in and through society and only indirectly bears on the state. Where the state attempts to deny this distinction, confrontation with the church will occur if the church is to remain true to its mission. But the church will endeavour to restore the distinction by continuing to serve the people in so far as it can and on the issues of justice by institutions like the Commission and *Moto* rather than by direct hierarchical intervention, although this may be necessary at times.

The relationship between church and society may be further clarified by remembering that while the church is a sign, instrument and partial realisation of the kingdom which Jesus came to inaugurate, it is not the kingdom either in its final eschatological form or in the fullness of its historical form here and now. The business of the church is to announce, discern and promote the kingdom wherever that is possible. It is in that spirit that the new stage in the church's work in Rhodesia should be understood. Given that self-understanding as servant of the kingdom and the freedom that goes with it, it may avoid the dilemma of attempting a parallel alternative political structure or of withdrawing to the sacristy. Whatever form the new Zimbabwe takes, these dilemmas and the strategies to overcome them will be crucial to the Church's effective mission of the gospel and of justice.

6.

Beyond a Purchased People

The angle of vision here will be that of emerging black consciousness of the deprivations suffered, of the need for
reform by having a more equitable share in the wealth
and power in Rhodesia to the point of aspiring to majority
(i.e. black) rule on the basis of one-man one-vote and of the
formation of a new (black-ruled) independent Zimbabwe.[1]
Again, it is not my purpose to write another historical account
of these events but to attempt a theological or faith understanding of them and to define theologically the place of the
church and its mission in the developing consciousness and
events.

It would be difficult to refute African criticism of the
original conjunction of political conquest and territorial/
mineral expropriation with the introduction of a Christian
gospel that depended on and at least implicitly endorsed
such conquest and expropriation. We have already examined
the dubious circumstances of the church's initial mission in
Rhodesia. And Europeans for whom historical hostilities
range from Northern Ireland to Greece and Turkey can
hardly afford to take a superior attitude to African invocation
of their own comparable memories or to the appeal to the
'Glorious Revolution' of 1893 or 1896 in recreating their
identity, establishing their dignity and promoting their movements for independence. The glib European response that
this part of Africa was conquered and reconquered many
times by varying African tribes who thus established a right
to rule by conquest, and that the European was simply the
latest, most effective and most enduring, is open to two

basic objections. Europeans have never simply accepted the right of conquest for their own territories in Europe. There is scarcely any simple analogy to the British Privy Council's resolution in 1918 about the right to rule Rhodesia as a right of conquest. And of course who can say what is enduring or when? If the right of conquest operated for the whites in 1918, why not for the blacks in 1980? At any rate such arguments and resolutions cannot finally settle the moral or political value of right of conquest. They do appear, in so far as they are endorsed by the church, to identify the church with a particular political position and a rather unsavoury one at that.

Yet moral and theological analysis cannot stop short with the identification of a past establishment of power as justified or unjustified and hold its breath until a new power-structure emerges. Within that new structure the church may continue its mission and its games of moral and theological analysis without having appropriated the lessons of the past or being prepared for the difficulties of the future. There is a permanent task of relating power and morality which the church and its theologians shirk at the cost of irrelevance to society and which they undertake at the cost of misunderstanding and even persecution. It is the second cost which the community claiming discipleship of Jesus Christ might be expected to be more ready to pay.

Historical Condition and Christian Faith

Perhaps the most illuminating way of understanding gospel and church from the African perspective may be to compare aspects of their historical condition with the more obvious gift and promise characteristics of Christian faith and try to analyse the actual and possible interactions.

These aspects and characteristics might be organised and presented in several ways. The complete presentation of them would demand detailed historical references to the actual conditions as well as detailed theological analysis of Christian faith and promise. As I have chosen very obvious and easily documented historical facts I will restrict the historical reference to a minimum. As I have already provided theological background I will be taking much of the earlier work for granted and trying to move into more concrete interaction and application.

Exclusion from Political City and Inclusion in City of God

The political exclusion of Africans from any share in governing the territory in which they lived is in retrospect the most striking feature of Rhodesian history from the African point of view. The details of it both in intent and content from the 1890s to the 1970s reveal a powerful, dynamic and fairly elaborate design on the part of successive white governments. The flirting with multi-racialism in the 1950s and the establishment of the Federation did not basically change the content and scarcely modified the intent. At any rate the rise of the Rhodesian Front and its unchallenged supremacy among the whites from 1964 reinforced both intent and content. The 'never in a thousand years' or 'not in my lifetime' declarations of an Ian Smith in the mid-seventies may have been the despairing rhetoric of the one-eyed king but it rang true for most of the blind he was leading. At least that is how it struck the excluded, the Africans themselves, as well as many outside observers.

Yet it would be impossible to assert a clear African consciousness of the nature and extent of that exclusion from a system that was in the beginning totally foreign to them. The rebellions, more richly symbolic today, the Bantu Voters' Associations and successive efforts to achieve some voice in the ordering at least of their own (restricted) affairs did gradually emerge as a demand for full inclusion in terms of one-man one-vote, majority rule, self-government and an independent Zimbabwe. In this process the problems of inclusion and exclusion began to be reversed. The question of how far whites would have a place in the new Zimbabwe arose in different fashions for both blacks and whites.

In all this period of course the Catholic church was, together with the other churches, continuing and extending its mission. It was gradually and then more rapidly (from the late forties) increasing its African membership. In this process the African people were offered full inclusion in the city of God though full inclusion in the city of man was denied then. In Jesus Christ all human beings are offered daughterhood and son-ship of the Father, sisterhood and brotherhood of one another. The barriers of division are broken down. There is no longer Jew or Gentile, slave or free, black or white. The family of the Father is all-inclusive and extends to all of humanity. This is of course both gift and promise. It is gift in history but suffers the limitations and ambiguities of history. It is promise of final, eschatological fulfilment in the age to come.

The inclusiveness of the Christian gospel, church and king-dom demolishes in principle all human and historical ex-clusiveness. How does it deal with it in practice? How did it deal with it in practice in the ninety years of Rhodesian white rule? Did it see the continuing political exclusion as a violation of Christian inclusiveness or as unrelated to it ('the church and the gospel are above politics') or as an inevitable and unchallengeable part of the ambiguity of human history to be overcome only at the final coming of the Lord? Clearly it is not possible to read the minds of the churchmen of these earlier or even later periods. Yet the prevailing theologies of the time and the actual record of events suggest certain tentative interpretations.

The church did not, at least for a considerable time, see the inclusivity of faith and salvation as challenging or in conflict with political exclusivity. This reflected current theology as well as cultural and political thinking about the distinction between religion and politics, the unreadi-ness of Africans for participation in the political process, the advantages which the introduction of European civilisation and political control offered the Africans as well as the impos-sibility of effectively challenging the European power struc-ture and the church's dependence on that structure to maintain law and order and so allow the church to carry on its mission. All this was of course supported by churchmen's belief that the divine inclusivity vastly exceeded in importance and effect any human and political exclusivity and in its ulti-mate eternal fulfilment more than compensated for the suffering and privations of this world.

In such a frame of reference the faith could easily, too easily perhaps, be seen as an endorsement of the political *status quo*, at least by relativising it as of no lasting significance. It would be fulfilling the opiate role attributed to it by Marx and others. Yet that hardly does full justice to other roles which it may have fulfilled and probably did. I have already mentioned something of the mediating and moderating role which the earlier mission church played, as between the colonial regime and the Africans. And in a situation of exclusion and privation which it felt powerless to change, the church could, although at the risk of misleading oppressor and oppressed, help people to endure the unendurable. This is not to excuse the failure to see the historical, political and material implications of divine inclusivity and its real incompatibility with the politics of exclusion. The gospel should have the effect of judging the self-centredness of the powerful and not just of consoling the powerless. It should provide the inspiration, courage and strength to understand and finally be seen to overcome the exclusion and discrimination. Its apparent failure to do so over such a long period is partly understandable in the human circumstances; it is hardly excusable to the church in the divine plan.

Earthly Privation and Heavenly Reward

The material poverty including poor health, educational and employment facilities, which characterised African living in contrast to the standards enjoyed by the white minority, raises the same kind of questions for church and gospel as political exclusion in relation to the inclusivity of salvation. The gospel might be and was used to relativise these earthly privations by comparison with the heavenly reward understood to await the 'blessed poor'. This in turn could and sometimes did become an encouragement to resignation for the poor Africans and endorsement of the *status quo* for the privileged Europeans. It took time for the church to realise that it could not endorse, much less approve such unjust distribution of earthly goods among people who were equal in the sight and power of God, and equally inheritors of the benefits of creation as well as salvation. Bishop Lamont's pastoral *A Purchased People* gave eloquent expression to the incompatibility between equality in the sight of God as affirmed in faith and gross inequalities in almost every human respect as practised in society.

Power, Dignity and Identity

The church's concept of mission emphasises the liberating and transforming power of the Spirit mediated through word and sacrament and community. The paradox of Christian history including the history of Jesus himself emphasises how far this divine power is operating through the apparently powerless, 'the foolish and weak of this world'. Rhodesia for ninety years might have offered a concrete and visible expression of the location of divine power as it is defined by this paradox. With that reversal of exclusivity-inclusivity which the paradox seems to demand, the Spirit clearly resided with the foolish and weak, the excluded — the Africans. To find God one had to search among them. The victims of human oppression are, by the standards of the Cross, the undeniable locus of divine presence.

I doubt if many Christians in Rhodesia really thought of the divine presence as located exclusively or even predominantly among the ignorant, uncivilised, poverty-stricken African masses. For one thing all the privileged whites were claiming to be Christian, indeed claiming to do what they did in the name of preserving Christian standards. And of course Christianity had been introduced by white missionaries enjoying the protection and some of the privileges of white power. The Christian communities were for a long time led by white Christians. Word, sacrament and formal Christian community depended on white leadership and initiative. To claim for deprived Africans even the primary location of God's presence sounds crazy, if not blasphemous, although one needs to remember that Calvary was hardly reasonable and the principal charge against the victim was blasphemy.

There are other difficulties. The exaltation of the victim can provide a convenient excuse for the persecutor and mislead Christian leaders into acceptance of the victimhood to be endured by others — the very reverse of Calvary in which Jesus as victim took on the sufferings of and for the others. Victimhood and powerlessness deriving from human injustice still cry to God for redress and it is the business of Christian leaders to hear and respond to that cry. The salvation made available through Calvary may not reach completion in history but it challenges and seeks to overcome sin in history, including the social sins of exclusion, discrimination and oppression of the powerless by the powerful. The overcoming of such sins demands a new distribution of power, an inclusion and participation in the power structure that prevents discriminating and oppressive relationships. Slowly and painfully Christians around the world and in Zimbabwe/Rhodesia have had to learn this.

Only with such power-sharing can people participate in shaping their own destiny in society and history. Such participation as subjects of their own history, personal and communal, is the obvious implication of their call to shape their eternal destiny manifest in Christ. It is the social and political expression of their gift and call as equal members of the created and redeemed family of the Father we call the human race. The emergence of an independent Zimbabwe inclusive of all its people is a salvific venture, however faulty and incomplete it will always remain.

Without that participation and sharing Rhodesian Africans felt for long second- or nth-class citizens. Their human and Christian dignity was impaired, ignored and at times totally denied. Shifted from place to place like animals to make room for developing/exploiting white projects, subjected to discriminating pass laws, carefully segregated in townships and Tribal Trust Lands, with their traditions ignored and communities broken, they were often made to feel inferior despite the apparent reassurance of the Christian message. Consciousness of their African dignity had to be reawakened and restored and not without peril for them and their white neighbours. Some of the peril of that reawakening is now being expressed in armed struggle. But the reawakening and restoration were essential to their healing and saving. They too have salvific dimensions.

The participation in power and the consciousness of dignity see integration and completion in a recovery and development of identity as individuals, African human beings and Christians. Personal identity is critical to the Christian understanding of the individual. God calls each one by name at baptism. It is in the development of that baptismal call that one grows up into the fullness of the person for which God has destined one. This occurs in and through community, human and Christian. The Christian is the completion and transformation of the human, not the denial of it, if one is to take the doctrines of creation, incarnation and resurrection seriously. Human identity as person in community is the preparation for and sharing in the divine fulfilment of salvation. The recovery and development of their identities as individual people with full names of their own, and as a people with their own tradition and destiny becomes part of the divine saving plan.

Expressions of Political Independence

As the black Rhodesians' demands crystallised, in the late fifties and early sixties, around the idea of national independence, two demands became symbolic of their total aspirations — 'majority rule' and 'one man, one vote'. By an irony, not unusual in the currents of history, they were adopting the tradition of their conqueror. Britain, as the colonising power, prides itself on its pioneering of parliamentary democracy and preservation of it. And these two slogans have emerged as somehow symbolic of such democratic government. The colonial settlers had in their restrictive tradition used this weapon of parliamentary democracy to wrest settler government and large-scale independence for Britain. But the 'one man, one vote' principle and the majority remained in white control. Voting laws were designed to have it so, permanently. More seriously, the view that the full Rhodesian population was peculiarly unready to share in government seemed to affect people even as critically aware as Bishop Lamont right into the 1970s.

Allowing for the manipulation by the white power-bloc of

the concept of parliamentary democracy and responsible government, we must respond to two questions which the use of these expressions or slogans involves. The first of these is a theological question. How far do 'one man, one vote' and 'majority rule' embody values of the kingdom? This question has to be taken further in asking how far these structures are necessary to becoming subject of one's own history, accepting responsibility by sharing in the decisions about one's destiny, ensuring protection of basic human rights and promoting justice and equality in distribution of goods, services and opportunities. In white-dominated Rhodesia before and after UDI the blacks were excluded from such participation. The obvious way in seemed to be by transfer of power and the way they were taught to achieve that was precisely through majority rule and one man, one vote. In that particular contest, the most human way of achieving their aspirations and realising kingdom values seemed to be through this mechanism. However, it remains no more than a mechanism although it may be an essential one in the circumstances of Rhodesia and many other countries.

The second, inevitable question is how far that mechanism may be adopted, will be necessary and will be basically respected after transfer of power and the gaining of independence. The examples of other African countries are mixed but so are those of countries with much longer conditions of parliamentary government including Britain itself, given its record in Northern Ireland. In any event other examples favourable or unfavourable provide no real guidance as to what will happen after independence in this particular country.

For Christians, in terms of political morality it should be said that there is nothing of itself sacred about the multi-party as opposed to the one-party system. How critics of the government and opponents of its policy are treated and find opportunity to promote peacefully alternative policies is a question to be faced in such situations. The history of some newly independent countries, with boundaries fixed in the interests of the colonial power and with tribal diversity often exploited by the same power, may demand strong and centralised government in the earlier stages of their independence.

The economic condition of the masses and the need for development may also encourage that policy. Both these considerations put at risk freedom for dissidents and also for critics.

In such a situation provisions for peaceful transfer of power must be attempted if one is to escape the abuses of dictatorship or the dangers of bloody coups. Basic human rights and respect for the role of law require careful monitoring. And the church will also have to fulfil its mission in this respect and use its prestige and international connections to protect the exploiter. Participation in government and fair sharing in goods and services will require adequate structures and dedicated people if a new power-bloc with a black face is not simply to replace the old. All these are tasks for Zimbabweans in the future Zimbabwe. There is no indication at present that they will perform their tasks less adequately than their predecessors or the white power-bloc. Observing previous 'white' standards, however, will not suffice to meet the needs of the people or justify the attempt to transfer power through armed rebellion. That justification must now be examined.

7.

The Armed Struggle

The original concern of this study was the war in Rhodesia and the problems it posed for Christians and churchmen. In the further development of the project it became clear that the war or violence could not be considered in isolation from the overall political situation out of which the war was born. The actual physical violence of the war had to have some kind of meaning or at any rate a context in which it could be judged as meaningful or meaningless and so evaluated morally. In the full sense that context is the whole history of Rhodesia, some of the salient factors of which we considered in the previous chapters. As I have already emphasised, this study is not a history of Rhodesia, not strictly the work of a historian. Yet the facts do matter although they may be difficult to establish and in their recounting inevitably bear the cast of the author's presuppositions, interests and biases. By now many of these should have become clear to the reader: my basic presupposition of Christian faith and its expression in the Catholic tradition, my professional interest in the moral dimension of social and political situations and events, my bias in favour of the deprived and exploited. There are others, consciously and some no doubt unconsciously held, which I cannot fully explore here. Yet they will not, I hope, prevent me from remaining faithful to the call to truth which is the fundamental presupposition of all academic work, Christian faith and social morality. Ever responsive to that call, one should exercise the self-criticism that prevents interest and bias, however powerful or respectable, from degenerating into self-indulgent apologetics, defending half-truths and sweeping aside all awkward facts and opinions.

Politics and Violence

As with so many words used widely in contentious circumstances, 'violence' tends to bear so many meanings that it may end up practically meaningless and useless in serious discussion. It is helpful therefore to repeat the primary meaning and first entry given to it in the Oxford English Dictionary. Violence is: 'The exercise of physical force so as to inflict injury on, or cause damage to, persons or property; action or conduct characterised by this; treatment or usage tending to cause bodily harm or forcibly interfering with personal freedom' (OED, Compact Form, 1971/9). Dictionary definitions (even in the OED) are not without their limitations and ambiguities. However, I will assume the general correctness of what we are offered here as providing a widely accepted and intelligible account of the usage of the word. Any extension or restriction of this usage will require separate justification. One obvious restriction required here is the qualification of violence as political. It is only in defence or pursuit of political goals that violence is our concern. Domestic violence, one of the most widespread forms in the western world, or violence associated with crimes against persons or property by individuals or groups for pleasure, gain, punishment or revenge is excluded from this study. Yet it must be acknowledged that clear-cut distinctions between political and other violence are not always easy to make and maintain. Violent robbery and kidnapping for ransom are sometimes given a political dimension by their agents. Political violence sometimes becomes a cover for settling old private scores or advancing one's personal fortune or cause. As political violence I shall be considering 'the exercise of physical force so as to inflict injury on, or cause damage to, persons or property' in order to maintain or destroy the existing political order.

In this sense politics is inextricably bound up with violence. Any political order one cares to mention has almost certainly been established by violence and is certainly maintained by at least the threat of it. The rule of law so beloved of the defenders of politics against men of violence depends on the sanction of physical force and its ability to inflict injury or cause damage. Much of the time that force may operate as a threat rather than an actuality but every state, whatever its civilised standards, is constantly called to go beyond the threat into the exercise. Political life and its moral assessment cannot ignore political violence. The task of moral assessment is to determine how far particular exercises of political violence are justified in any particular set of circumstances. The wider context of this discussion I have dealt with in an earlier chapter. The more demanding consideration of the particular circumstances of Rhodesia provides the current task.

Politics and Violence in Rhodesia

In the light of the historical link between politics and force or violence, the moralist and the church must continually face two questions: How is force or the threat of force being used to establish or maintain a certain political order? What kind of political order is being established or maintained? The first question emphasises the pervasiveness of force in political life but allows for different forms of its exercise and for the justification of some of these. The second is a more fundamental question. It includes the question about just cause expressed in the traditional discussion of just war or revolution, embraces at the same time the state's use of force outside war or revolution, and allows for supplements or alternatives to force in any or all of these situations. At least by returning to these questions these dimensions of the situation can be dealt with in a way free from some of the emotional disturbance which too often accompanies discussions of violence. At the same time the repetition of these questions permits escape from the historical wrangling of who started what and when, while ensuring that history is taken seriously by asking the questions in the different historical contexts. This is particularly important in Rhodesia — and in Northern Ireland also — where people frequently get confused about who did what in 1890, 1893, 1896, 1961, 1965, 1969, 1972, 1979. These and other dates are all important and the questions about force and the political order have to be asked anew in connection with many of them but only so that by asking and answering them effectively in the present, they may provide some guidance for more appropriate action in the future.

How is Force Being Exercised?

This study was begun in the middle of a war and is being completed with the war still in progress. Its original impetus came from priests and others caught in the middle of war who were anxious for help in evaluating the morality of various situations which the war involved. The generally close connection between politics, force, violence and war has been particularly true of Rhodesia in the ninety years of its history. The question, how is force being used, might have been asked at any one of the dates listed above or indeed at any time during that ninety years. To ask it first at this time is to address the most immediate concerns of many people undergoing the effects of the war. It enables one to move through the different levels of moral assessment necessary, from the more immediate to the more fundamental. It offers one way of evaluating the past without becoming paralysed by it. It could continue to be of service in the future as the maintenance of any new order will involve the use of force and that in turn will require to be monitored and evaluated. Attempts in the future to displace any existing order may result in new wars and the uncertain situation to the south of the new Zimbabwe, in South Africa, may draw the new nation into protracted border warfare as South Africa's guerillas or security forces move back and over across the Limpopo. For the people caught in the middle of these situations, the villagers, the farmers, the medical workers, the clergy and all the other unarmed citizens, the immediate question of what kind of violence this is or how force is being used here will continue to press upon them, requiring practical responses from people without the time or opportunity to explore the deeper questions.

Combatants and Non-combatants

In attempting to evaluate morally the use of force in a war-situation such as that in Rhodesia, a primary consideration is the distinction between combatants and non-combatants. In so far as war has been morally justified, traditional analysis has insisted on the observance of this distinction in the conduct of the war. Without it no limitations on the conduct of war are possible. If the moral rationale for war is the maintenance or establishment of a political order and structure, the first requirement of such an order is that it protect the human person and human life. Without such a commitment the order itself is immoral, indeed is really disorder, and ultimately not viable. Both the armed upholders of the existing order in Rhodesia and its armed opponents would claim to be defending or promoting an order in which such respect for human person and life are accepted. Their armed efforts must take account therefore of this use of force as exceptional, demanded by unusual circumstances, to be regretted, and to be pursued reluctantly. Killing even in pursuit of such order cannot be easily justified because it appears to clash with the very heart of such order, respect for the human person and life. Clearly the justification of such activity cannot be extended beyond the armed opponents themselves. The very young, the very old, the sick are by definition excluded from the ranks of the armed opponents. So are very many people both by choice and necessity. However, the burden of proof as to who are non-combatants does not lie with the non-combatants themselves. People of all ranks and ages are to be presumed non-combatant unless they give real indications to the contrary. Unless this presumption is primary the distinction may well be accepted in theory; it will be denied in practice.

The acceptance in theory or at least the public statement of this distinction is affirmed whenever it seems to be most outrageously violated in practice, whether by attributing the violation to the other side or by claiming that those subjected to the violence were combatants, a military target. The many disputes about the deaths of black villagers in the

Tribal Trust Lands, or of white missionaries in some of the more remote missions, exemplify this contradiction between the claims of the two sides. Whether a particular incident is finally assessed as the work of the guerrillas or the work of the security forces, there are sufficient incidents and sufficient evidence to make it absolutely clear that the distinction between combatant and non-combatant is frequently ignored in practice by both, and that indiscriminate killing of a kind that is morally indefensible, whatever the cause espoused, is widespread. On the facts and morality of this issue Christians and their leaders should be clear. The complexity of guerrilla war on both sides, and the complexity of the Rhodesian war in particular, can make it difficult to distinguish combatant and non-combarant. Such complexity does not provide adequate excuse for the many well-documented instances of black tribesmen being arbitrarily and freely killed — such as the fifty to a hundred caught in cross-fire at Gutu in May 1978 (without a single member of the Security Forces or the guerrillas presumably engaged in the cross-fire being killed). Other cases were the notorious shooting down of the civilian aircraft (admitted by the ZAPU), and the killing of white missionaries such as Bishop Schmitt and his companions (widely attributed to the guerrillas but denied by them).

The attitude of Defence Minister P. K. van der Byl as expressed in parliament, 'as far as I am concerned the more curfew breakers that are shot the better' (July 1975)[1] reveals something of the attitude of the Smith regime to the need to uphold the distinction between combatants and non-combatants. His later assertion (18 August 1976) that 'the overwhelming majority [of curfew breakers shot] had been proved beyond any doubt to have been assisting terrorists in one way or another'[2] does not bear serious examination in view of the cases listed for example in the Justice and Peace Report, *Civil War in Rhodesia* (London 1976). The government's introduction of the Indemnity and Compensation Act, 1975, which had retrospective effect back to 1 December 1972, gave the state, its employees and appointees immunity from criminal and civil court action for harm done 'in good faith' to suppress terrorism or to maintain public order. This was really in response to an earlier document of the Justice and Peace Commission, *The Man in the Middle* (1975), which produced evidence to show that torture, ill-treatment and destruction of property had been used by the Security Forces against innocent civilians. Not only was the government violating the distinction between combatant and non-combatant; it was, despite earlier protestations that the courts were open to anybody who had a complaint, ruling out the possibility of any such remedy and in effect admitting the truth of the Commission's claims.

The reported treatment by the guerrillas of those suspected of being 'sell-outs' or informers or of engaging in witch-craft for example as well as their treatment of families of white farmers confirmed on the other side how far the distinction between combatants and non-combatants was disappearing in practice. The use of landmines resulting in the deaths of many villagers revealed at least a carelessness about the distinction. The terrorising of whole villages and areas by both security forces and guerrillas, the breakdown of discipline and the emergence of marauding bands, the disputes between rival groups of guerrillas, the emergence after the March Settlement of 1978 of private armies loyal to the different internal leaders, and the extension of martial law to almost the whole country in late 1978 and early 1979 — all these intensified the violence considerably and particularly the threat to the black civilian population. The death-rate or body-count increased to the point where only very rough estimates are available. The extension of the war beyond Rhodesia into Zambia and Mozambique, however justified militarily by the security forces, led inevitably to increased death and suffering for non-combatant refugees. The recent course of the war looks more like an exercise in competitive terror in which each side tries to destroy the morale and support of the other by terrorising the civilian population. If either side is to make any credible claims for the justice of its campaign it must learn to respect and protect the lives and rights of civilians. The first duty of moral leaders is to insist on this distinction, to denounce its violations on both sides, to seek preventive and protective measures even at risk to themselves. Such limitation of the war is not easy but it is a first claim on moral conscience, witness and service to protect the innocent and promote some hope of a future moral political order.

Torture, Inhuman and Degrading Treatment

Apart from the actual killing of combatants and non-combatants, the war in Rhodesia, like so many others, has a history of treatment of prisoners and suspects which violates the rights defined in the UN Declaration of Human Rights as accepted, if not always respected, by most countries today. Article 5 of the Declaration states: No one shall be subjected to torture or to cruel, inhuman or degrading treatment or punishment.

In the Rhodesian situation there is no doubt, as we shall see, that this article has been frequently and seriously violated. The terrorising of the population by guerrillas in the TTLs by beatings, rape, abduction of the young and wanton destruction of property undoubtedly happens if reliable witnesses from the population themselves and the serving missionaries are to be believed. How widespread this is, what proportion of guerrilla activity it constitutes, how far it is deliberate policy and how far due to the indiscipline of particular groups or to a more widespread breakdown in discipline, it is impossible on the evidence available to assess. Inhuman and degrading treatment including cruel punishments such as cutting off lips and ears forms a part of the guerrilla action and must be condemned and opposed where possible. The needs of warfare or the pressure of guerrilla warfare may simply not be invoked to excuse such barbarous behaviour. Endorsement of it as a policy or acceptance of it as a regrettable necessity without any attempt to curtail it or discipline the offenders would again undercut the claim to be fighting for a just and humane society. The means employed enter closely into the end to be achieved in political affairs, and a society with respect for human life and dignity cannot be built by means which totally ignore that respect.

The torture and inhuman and degrading treatment inflicted by the security forces are at least as well established. The work of the Justice and Peace Commission provides two outstanding and well researched documents on the treatment by the security forces of black civilians. *The Man in the Middle* and *Civil War in Rhodesia,* referred to earlier, leave very little doubt about the existence and extent of torture and the like in dealing with black suspects against whom little evidence could be mustered and no charges were subsequently brought. Any little doubt there might have been was certainly eroded by the action of the government in promising investigation and then refusing it, in maintaining that the courts were open and then introducing the Indemnity and Compensation Act, in preferring charges against members of the Justice and Peace Commission and then dropping them.

Apart from the appalling cases of personal ill-treatment and torture which are well established, systematic ill-treatment of large groups of the civilian population is also evident. The forcible removal of large sections from their home areas to areas sometimes hundreds of miles away in the interests of prosecuting the war more firmly or even, it is sometimes suggested, of protecting the civilians themselves, has led to untold hardship. The creation of the protected villages was a more sophisticated application of the same policy and frequently led to even more suffering. The people were separated from their homes, land, cattle and crops; they were also limited as to the time and freedom needed to attend to these, and they often endured privation and harassment within the 'protected villages' themselves. The scale of suffering which this policy produced for the helpless African is enormous.

The inhumanity of the war as practised by both sides had a multiplier effect due to the competitive pressure on the civilians in the war areas to cooperate with one side and so be punished by the other. The mere presence — or even suspected presence — of one side in the recent past was sufficient warrant for the other to take punitive action in a morally indefensible fashion, although again, arguing on some basis of the necessity of the war, both sides are as quick to defend their own actions as they are to attribute the obviously heinous to the other side.

Summary Evaluation of how Force is used in the Rhodesian War

The first question arising in a war situation is how force is being exercised with particular reference to the distinction between combatants and non-combatants and the use of torture or inhuman and degrading treatment. This constitutes the first question because the war is going on and people need some help in assessing how it is going. It is not the final question and does not answer the question how far the war is justified at all for either side. It tries to deal with the most immediate question. The reasons alleged for the war enter into the answer in so far as they offer some guideline as to the war-makers' criteria for justified action. Where those criteria involve the defence or establishment of a just society with respect for all human persons, the elimination or ignoring of the distinction between combatant and non-combatant, and the use of torture, contradict the aims alleged to justify the war. Appeals to such self-contradiction may help to restrain the war-makers and to clarify particular incidents for the morally concerned. They may also help to expose for what they are the specious excuses by which the agents of atrocities justify themselves, saying that their action is necessary to secure the greater good or else is to be seen as among the inevitable mistakes always made in time of war. More profoundly this evaluation rests on a sense of the dignity of the human being and the value of his life as that has emerged in the Christian and, also, in the wider, human tradition. Without denying that part of their tradition which has for so long recognised the possibility of a just war, Christians can offer some discriminating help on what is certainly not tolerable in war, if it is to be just in its manner and not merely in its aim.

What Kind of Political Order is being Defended or Established?

In the moral tradition of the just war the first condition

usually stated is that the cause should be just. In the present context that may be translated as the defence (by the security forces) or the establishment (by the guerrilla forces) of a particular political order. Obviously the political orders involved are (understood to be) mutually exclusive. They are intimately related in that one is in some sense the opposite of the other. At least important aspects of the one are excluded by the other. In the same tradition, change of control of the political structure would not rank as a sufficient cause. Control must be bound up with issues more fundamental to the structure of society, for example, respect for basic human rights, equality of all before the law, freedom from arbitrary arrest and imprisonment, participation by all in the governance of society. Such serious political change which would amount to a movement from an oppressed society to a free one would not automatically justify war but it could satisfy the first condition in the traditional analysis. The question to be asked of both the security forces and the guerrillas then is: are they seeking to defend/establish a free and just society or an oppressive and unjust one? While that question is basic and the answers to be expected from spokespeople on both sides predictable, some further teasing out is necessary before any kind of fair and objective answers can be given by people with the responsibility of moral leadership.

What are the Security Forces defending?

Given the early history of Rhodesia, its developments after the coming to power of the Rhodesian Front, UDI and the 1969 Constitution, certain glib answers to this question will not do. To invoke simply the authority of the state in the wake of UDI or the defence of Christian values and civilised standards after a long history of their neglect and violation does not convince a fair-minded observer. A more persuasive answer in the light of the historical use of force, legislation and economic power is the defence of white power and privilege. The practice and the rhetoric of the Smith government of 1964, and indeed of many of its predecessors, scarcely bears any other reasonable interpretation. It might, however, be qualified by appealing to the economic and other achievements of the whites which would be lost to the blacks also, if the whites were simply to leave the country or hand over power thoughtlessly to the first group of armed blacks to appear on the scene. In this sense the security forces' defence activity might be directed to achieving an orderly reform of the structure and an orderly transfer of power to the people as a whole. That this was far from the minds of the leaders, political and military, is clear from the language and behaviour they employed right up to the time when a combination of external pressures, economic difficulties and military problems brought them to the negotiating table. How far, even then, they were ready for genuine reform and sharing of power may be deduced from the inherent limitations of the internal settlement of 3 March 1978. That settlement will demand fuller consideration later; its relevance here lies in the light it throws on the action of the security forces as preparing the way for effective and organised change to a society free from the injustice, discrimination and oppression which had marked Rhodesia for so long.

Although the answer that the security forces were really fighting to protect white power and privilege remains more likely than that it was preserving the existing order to allow for change, other considerations do arise. Self-interest, the examples of Mozambique and Angola and acceptance by the guerrillas of help from such communist countries as Russia and China supported a view long cherished by white Rhodesians that they were fighting a war against communism and against a communist take-over of Southern Africa. Communist support for the guerrillas certainly exists; their leaders at least in the person of Robert Mugabe harbour some socialist and even Marxist ideas. How far these amount to a communist ideology or would make their movements instruments of an external communist take-over is unclear. This interpretation of their position would come more persuasively from the whites if it did not coincide so totally with their own self-interest, if they had not dismissed as communism all demands for justice and the development of black nationalism which Rhodesia shared with the rest of Africa in the 1950s and 1960s and if they were even now ready to make a genuine and generous settlement with the internal leaders.

A more acceptable argument for at least some defensive activity by the security forces would be the protection of white lives and the prevention of anarchy which might develop if they were simply to lay down their arms. This danger has been aggravated by the divisions among the guerrillas themselves based on tribal, personal and ideological reasons, by the increase in banditry which a war inevitably encourages and by the growth of the private armies fostered by the white and internal black leaders. However such defensive action would only make real sense where other steps were being taken to bring the war as a whole to an end by serious negotiation and readiness for radical change.

In summary, the society which, up to 3 March 1978, the security forces were defending, was not the kind of just and free society that would satisfy the first condition in the just war tradition. That condition could only be justified where something clearly worse — such as sheer anarchy — would follow and where the political masters of the military were committed to the establishment of a genuinely just society and not merely defence of the status quo. The internal settlement has changed the situation. The security forces now, at least nominally, fight under a black prime minister with a majority of blacks in parliament. Questions remain about how real the transfer of power has been and how far, therefore, discrimination is being removed and about how far the internal settlement has been accepted by an informed black population. While the whites were given a referendum on the settlement, the blacks were not. The blacks opposed to the election did not get a chance to put forward their views at election time and there are doubts about how far those who voted were acting freely. The retention of control over the security forces, the judiciary and the civil services together with economic power in white hands and the continuing role of people like Ian Smith and P. K. van der Byl suggests to many observers a form of black-wash, putting a black face on the old white power-reality. If this is in fact true or at any rate the intention of the white leaders, political and military, then the cause they are defending is no more just than it was. If in reality and intention genuine movement is taking place towards a just society, then the situation is changed and the society which the guerrillas have been attacking and that which they have been seeking to establish have entered a new phase. It is necessary at this stage to put our second question to the guerrillas.

What are the Guerrillas Attacking and what are they Seeking to Establish?

In the light of the foregoing discussion of the society being defended by the security forces, the fair answer to the question posed to the guerrillas — at least as far as what they are attacking is concerned — might seem obvious: the oppressive society of Rhodesia as developed to its fullness under the Rhodesian Front government. There is clearly much truth in this answer and given the seriousness and persistence of the oppression it might be considered to satisfy the first condition of the just war tradition (although not necessarily the others). Two further problems require discussion however. What do the guerrilla leaders intend to replace it with; what are they seeking to establish? And how far are they motivated by considerations of personal power and privilege and how far are they genuinely committed to the good of the people?

The first of these questions cannot be answered with complete precision even by the leaders themselves. Some outline of the answer is contained in what they oppose, the racist and oppressive regimes of Rhodesia. After that they tend invariably to be vague. Joshua Nkomo does not appear to have a concept of society that goes beyond the non-racial, self-governing model hitherto excluded in Rhodesia. His views on economic organisation in so far as they are known seem to be some kind of modified capitalism. Both leaders and movements affirm their respect for whites and the contribution they can make to free Zimbabwe. Whatever the defects of their announced programmes they do not include racialism. Robert Mugabe espouses a more socialist line with definite Marxist implications on the ownership of the means of production and a radical redistribution of land and other forms of wealth. So far as it goes on paper it suggests some kind of combination of African tradition and socialist economics. It may properly be considered frightening by those who have benefited from the previous extraordinary unjust distribution of wealth but it is hard to maintain at this stage that the Mugabe proposals should be regarded as immoral. What might happen in practice to extend or attenuate such proposals is anybody's guess and no clear conclusions can be drawn from the experience of either Mozambique or Angola. In both instances much more clearly ideological movements came to power while the economic structure was entirely different. That serious economic change has to take place and that the one-party state so common in Africa may also be introduced does not make the positive programmes of Mugabe or Nkomo, in so far as they are clearly developed, unacceptable bases for the introduction of a just society.

It may be of course that their personal intentions or their commitments to external socialist powers in Russia or China, Cuba or East Germany go much further, and in the direction of a new oppression and injustice, than is now clear. The evidence for that is tenuous at best. In face of the existing injustices in Rhodesia it sounds too much like the traditional rationalisations of the white power-structure. If it were true it would seriously diminish the guerrillas' claim to be espousing a just cause, although many might fairly claim that they were dealing with obvious, existing injustice and that they were not to be distracted from that by the concealed and destructive aims of some of their leaders. For good or ill is clearly uncertain in any movement for independence, particularly one engaged in guerrilla warfare. The history of fragmentation in the Zimbabwean independence movement offers ample evidence of this, making it all the more difficult to draw any clear-cut conclusions about the shape of the future Zimbabwe should these movements in fact come to power.

Closely connected with fragmentation is the problem of personal power-seeking among the leaders themselves.It would be unfair to characterise this as peculiar to Zimbabweans, Africans or even politicians engaged in the hazardous task of campaigning for independence and self-government. Yet it has a close bearing on these. The pressure of underground and exile politics which is all Rhodesian Africans enjoyed for so long exaggerates differences of ideology, strategy, even tribal and personal loyalty. Some personal authority and power may be useful to weld the diverse elements together — only to result in other divisions. The uneasy alliance of Nkomo and Mugabe, as it appears, and the breakdown of the alliance between Muzorewa and Sithole are but the latest manifestations of a long-standing problem. In such circumstances it is hard even for the particular leader to distinguish between personal need for power with the demand for personal loyalty and basic commitment to the social good. A recent instance of that difficulty occurred in the quite different circumstances of President Carter and his cabinet (July 1979). And it would apply as much to the internal leaders, Muzorewa and Sithole as to Nkomo and Mugabe. Arguments of the kind that Muzorewa and Sithole accepted the Internal Settlement as their only way to power because they did not command any guerrillas, or that Nkomo and Mugabe will not accept because they seek personal power through the guerrillas, tend to cancel out in the absence of clear evidence. It may, however, be maintained that in so far as individual leaders place personal power ahead of their commitment to the emergence of a just society in Rhodesia and make that personal power the decisive basis for their action, they have undermined the justice of their cause and no longer satisfy the first condition. However, personal ambition and desire for power is a regular part of political motivation; what matters is that it should not be the decisive or the only one.

What are the Alternatives to Force?

That force should respect in its exercise the basic distinction between combatants and non-combatants and that, in its treatment of both, it should avoid the excessive and degrading activity discussed and that it be excercised for a basically moral cause, all this does not automatically justify it. In traditional language it may be invoked only as a last resort. There must be no other alternatives available. The reasoning behind this condition rests on the increase in suffering and destruction which force always involves and the obligation to avoid this unless it is absolutely necessary in order to overcome the suffering and destruction which already by definition exist or will exist in the society to be destroyed or to be established.

In the history of Rhodesia the white governments and their supporters had many opportunities to alleviate the injustices endured by the Africans. From the 1920s at least, African organisations such as the Rhodesian Bantu Voters Association, concerned with political reform, or the Commercial and Industrial Union of African workers, offered obvious points of contact and negotiation for reform and integration in limited and non-threatening ways. Some outstanding missionaries like Shirley Cripps and White and their supporters overseas as well as the interests of the Colonial Office in London encouraged and indicated this way of reform. Effectively these offers were rejected. Their renewal after World War II and their expression through strike action like that of 1948 seemed merely to harden the hearts of the whites. The brief flirtation with partnership in the days of Federation in the late fifties could not endure the mildly reformist attitudes of Garfield Todd as Prime Minister. And the emergence of Black Nationalism in Africa generally — and so in Rhodesia — together with the need to organise politically for genuine self-government by all the people of Rhodesia met with the by now familiar pattern of response: police attacks on meetings, the banning of a succession of parties, the arrest and detention of black leaders, all accompanied by a growing array of emergency law and order administration. The culmination of all this in the rise of the Rhodesian Front, the coming to power of Ian Smith, the development of UDI and the 1969 Constitution and Land Act proved the definitive rejection by the Rhodesian white leaders of any fair and negotiated settlement. The reforms which the blacks sought and which were clearly overdue were not the subject of negotiation and the Rhodesian Front did not seriously entertain any strategies other than force in their response to the claims, now largely seen to be just, of the African majority. Force was for them much more a first than a last resort.

The fact that the Rhodesian Front resorted mainly to force and ignored other opportunities does not mean that the proponents of change were automatically bound or justified in following the same pattern. The history of authoritarian governments suggests that their first resort will be force although their last may be negotiation and sometimes the humiliating negotiation of flight as was the case with the Somoza regime in Nicaragua. However the final negotiation — and even departure — of their leaders is not necessarily achieved by counter-force. India is an outstanding example of that. And even if the weight of historical example is against the Indian model, the development of philosophy and strategy by Gandhi has opened up new possibilities of resisting and overcoming unjust regimes whose first resort is to reach for the gun. In the 1960s much of British Africa reached independence in relatively peaceful fashion. It is clear that Rhodesian Africans thought that they could and would follow this pattern. They regarded the British as the responsible colonial power which would stand by its commitments and ensure their status in an independent Rhodesia. As they gradually realised that the British were not, for a mixture of reasons, going to stand firm, the main plank of their alternative policy to violence was taken away. Their own efforts at constitutional-political activity and at socio-economic pressure produced inevitably repressive effects of emergency legislation, banning and detention as we have seen. A sophisticated non-violent resistance movement would have anticipated such a reaction and made plans to deal with it. In Rhodesia in the 1960s this was unrealistic. Very little reflection on the Gandhi philosophy and technique — or development of it — had occurred outside the civil rights movement of the United States. An attempt later in the decade to introduce it into

Northern Ireland perished before the violent repressive actions of the security forces and the consequent reassertion of the old Irish physical violence tradition. People who might have been expected to give a lead in this area, the Christian communities and their leaders, were not yet politically aware enough to analyse the situation in Rhodesia or to recognise their responsibility to help provide alternatives to the violence they were often so quick to denounce. Yet the resort to violence in the sixties was fitful and clearly unsuccessful. The Home-Smith proposals in 1971 and the arrival of the Pearce Commission inspired the Africans to a united and sophisticated non-violent resistance movement which convinced a by no means sympathetic commission that the settlement was not acceptable to them. That moment and movement were never recaptured and the struggle took on for the guerrillas and the security forces a definitive armed character from December 1972. External non-violent pressure through boycott and economic sanctions had by then proved their inadequacy, partly due to the resourcefulness of the Rhodesian whites but mainly to the cooperation of South Africa and the fraudulent behaviour of many states officially committed to sanctions, including in the case of oil Britain, the original proponent of sanctions, against whose government Rhodesia was in revolt. The shabby story of the busting of the oil-sanctions with government connivance reaching apparently to the very top has rightly damaged British and western credibility among Africans, to an unknown but enormous degree. It was at least a significant factor in the decision of the Rhodesian whites not to negotiate and to use only the language of force. Directly and indirectly it pushed the Africans more surely in the direction of an armed response.

Without preparation, leadership and real external support in terms of publicity and genuine economic sanctions; and faced with a ruthless and unyielding regime, it is difficult to see how non-violent resistance could have been sustained and developed in Rhodesia in the sixties and seventies. The alternatives were to wait for the sanctions to work, increasingly unlikely given the cheating that went on; to hope for a British intervention, unrealistic after UDI was allowed to pass by; to endure without resistance what black Rhodesians had endured for so long, an unlikely outcome in view of the changed psychological attitude within Rhodesia, and the changed social and political attitudes and events throughout much of Africa, or finally to meet force with force. Various Rhodesian Africans made different choices and some (most perhaps) were not even aware that they had a choice at all. A growing number opted for the armed struggle and in so far as the two critical conditions of the just war doctrine are concerned – a proportionately serious just cause and no other means to achieve this available – it would be hard to fault them morally. How far, once that decision was taken or occurred, the war really was just depends a good deal on the answers to the question examined earlier on how the war was and is conducted. The large measure of injustice in the conduct of the war by the guerrillas has already been discussed. And it could amount to a total invalidation of the claim to be fighting a just war.

The other difficulty of how far the Internal Settlement has rendered the war unnecessary and so immoral will not easily go away either. Given the limitations of the settlement, already treated, it is reasonable and moral for the guerrillas and their leaders not to hand in their arms until it is absolutely clear that a radical change has taken place and that they are not going to be cheated once again by the deviousness and cleverness of Smith and his men. That seems to be the prudent attitude of President Carter and other world leaders in their approach to the removal of economic sanctions and granting of recognition. It is hardly too much to allow the guerrillas and their leaders who have suffered so much, whose efforts helped bring Smith to negotiate in the first place and who have everything to lose by precipitate action now.

Force of Violence and the Christian

Some readers may be surprised at my apparent easy acceptance of the just war theory, still more at the manner of my application of it to the war in Rhodesia and perhaps still more at my refusal to invoke gospel values in presenting my moral analysis. I might plead in defence my earlier extensive discussion of gospel or kingdom values in relation to politics and to the use of force or violence in particular. Yet some further reflection is called for here. The just war tradition grew up in a Christian context. Its first exponents were Ambrose and Augustine. In recent times it has moved through various fashionable shifts from outright rejection in the name of the Christian commitment to pacifism to the endorsement no longer of inter-state wars but of wars of independence against oppressive regimes. I believe that a two-level approach for Christians at this stage in history is important. The tradition itself with appropriate adaptation to our circumstances (in regard to nuclear weapons for example) provides a useful tool of analysis and discrimination where war actually exists such as Rhodesia for example or, very recently, Nicaragua, or where it seems in danger of occurring in the near future. In these situations where alternatives cannot be provided in time, moral monitoring in the fashion outlined earlier is, I believe, essential in order to humanise the war, allow people to make serious judgments about it and so reduce some of its worst features as well as providing a stimulus and perhaps criteria for a finally just settlement. As so much of the globe is potentially exposed to this kind of armed conflict or is enduring armed oppression of a most destructive kind, it would be abdication of their responsibility for Christians and moralists not to tackle these problems.

It remains true and is strongly emphasised in the tradition that armed response should be a very reluctant and last resort. It has also become true in our own time that we have learned more deeply the horrors of war and are no longer tempted to glorify it as that tradition from Aristotle to some modern churchmen did. More importantly we are developing a set of international institutions, still woefully inadequate, which will in the long run, we hope, allow intra- and inter-state crimes and disputes of a political nature to be settled by a fair and accepted process. That is still a long way off but it can and must be brought nearer if the human race is to be released from the continuing suffering of war.

These ideas and ideals found expression in the teaching and life of Gandhi in this century when he introduced us to a new horizon of human possibility in his programme of *satyagraha, ahimsa* and *Ashram.* This was adapted success- fully to the very different situation of the United States by Martin Luther King and his followers. It clearly influenced Bishop Muzorewa in his organisation of the campaign against the Home-Smith proposals. It is along this line that Christians must work specifically today. However much gospel and kingdom values may be implicitly tolerant of the limited use of force outlined above, it is a choosing of the lesser evil and leaves a tendency to repeat itself. To overcome even that lesser evil (which is still very great) and to prevent the chain reaction to which history is witness, Christians should look at the more explicit gospel and kingdom values which Gandhi and his successors have expounded. If the church is to take seriously its newly discovered political role of discerning and promoting in society the values of the kingdom, there is no better place to begin than with the development of strategies for peaceful change through studying and employing the philosophy, discipline, spirituality and strategy of Gandhi, King and others. This seems to me a peculiarly Christian call today and particularly so in areas like Southern Africa and Northern Ireland. To many people in Rhodesia it may seem too late. In an obvious sense it is. Yet such a commitment can help to reduce violence now by attracting young people into an effective alternative and by achieving certain gains of its own for which violence is no longer necessary. Mugabe for example made it clear that his movement welcomed any initiative assisting in the emergence of a just, non-racial society. And it would be hard to see any committed leader of the Africans objecting to or interfering with such initiatives. They could vary from simple local development projects to the ever-necessary work of Justice and Peace in monitoring the behaviour of guerrillas and security forces and so to more organised resistance to and prevention of atrocities by any of the many armed groups in the country.

Conclusions. Theological, Pastoral and Personal

Aim and Audience

This study was undertaken as both an intellectual and a pastoral task. By that I mean that I sought to investigate and clarify as rigorously as I could the relationship between church and politics as it emerges today in Christian, more specifically Catholic, theology and to understand and illuminate the Rhodesian situation in the light of that theological inquiry. But I was doing this, not as an interesting intellectual exercise, which it was, but as a way of helping church and Christians, primarily in Rhodesia but also in the world at large. I wanted to help them to find the best pastoral response in difficult, delicate and constantly changing political circumstances. How far I may have succeeded or failed does not rest entirely with me. The obvious limitations of my work will certainly affect its usefulness. But a book like this is not a theological cook-book with easily found and readily applicable recipes appropriate to different occasions. As any theological book should be, it is for critical appropriation (or rejection) as a way of developing one's horizons of understanding and skills of evaluating and responding. It is only by critical dialogue with such a book that its intellectual merit can be measured and assimilated, its pastoral value incorporated in Christian practice. These responsibilities rest with the readership. Banal as such reflection must appear, it seemed to me necessary to express it, firstly as a tribute to the many people who helped me to write this book in the first place. However inadequately I may have mediated their reflection on and concern with these issues, I would hope readers would respect and grapple with the same issues. Secondly I found this a very difficult book to write. And while I can hardly expect a prospective reader to be moved by sympathy for my difficulties in the writing, I am more convinced after my own struggle with the many authors I read in preparing this study, that easy reading is not usually very helpful reading. My struggle with much of the theological and Rhodesian material in this book will be obvious in the writing. To share whatever insight I eventually achieved and, better still, to go beyond it in understanding and practice, the reader must also struggle at times. If she/he has struggled this far she/he will already know this but may be consoled by the thought that serious reading, like serious writing, is difficult. Perhaps Thomas Mann's dictum that the good writer is somebody who finds it very hard to write might be adapted to describe the good reader as somebody who finds it very hard to read but still, like the writer, perseveres.

Method and Structure

The table of contents, the introduction and the book itself reveal a method and structure that do not cease to be applicable, I believe, when the writing or reading of the book is completed. Given its search for understanding and pastoral strategy in changing political circumstances, the church has to move through a continuing cycle of interpretation or understanding and response, changing interpretation and changing response. At both the level of the universal church and that of the local church this mutual interchange between theology (theory) and practice (pastoral) expands the church's understanding and enriches its pastoral response. The further interchange between the universal and the local church encourages and enables continuing mutual enrichment in theological understanding and pastoral response. This of course could and does occur between particular local churches such as the churches in Rhodesia and Ireland or Rhodesia and South Africa. The growth of such interchange between local churches has become a feature of the post-Vatican II era. National and regional conferences of bishops already express this but geography is not the only basis for fruitful contact and exchange. Such exchange should be mutual and both critical and sympathetic. Simple uncritical borrowing of ideas or practices from Latin America to Africa or Asia, for example, is no more helpful than was the wholesale, thoughtless transplanting of European ideas and practices to these areas in the past. The value of the ideas of there being only one earth, or of our forming a global village, must not be allowed to obscure the rich diversity of that earth or of the human achievements and needs of so many different peoples and cultures. To foster diversity in unity is part of the challenge of the church's faith in the creativity and fatherhood of the God of Jesus Christ.

Churches are not only diverse in geography, cultural background, political and social structures and problems. As churches they have different rhythms of development, with a different *kairos*, or succession of *kairoi*, perhaps best rendered as the timing of the Spirit. The prayerful and skilful discerning of the timing of the Spirit constitutes a continuing and difficult task for each church and indeed every Christian. The analysis offered in this book is intended as a help in developing the skills required in one aspect of the church's mission — that is, its interaction with the political situation and its promotion of social justice and the other values of the kingdom.

However helpful outsiders and exchange with other churches may be in describing and defining the skills involved, only the particular church can finally discern its own *kairos* and, in this complex and sinful world, with difficulty and, at most, partial success. Even such partial success is important, and not just to that particular church in devising its response. It also enters the wider heritage of other churches and the church universal. The further sensitivity of all of us to the timing of the Spirit and our response to it is enriched or enfeebled by the achievements of other churches and other Christians. Solidarity in diversity, support in our different situations, awareness of our diverse *kairoi* should characterise the Christian community as a whole. The achievements in discernment and response of the Rhodesian church at this crucial time have significance for all of us and call for our support in the sharing of prayer, skills and experiences. From the Rhodesian church's negotiation of its *kairoi*, the British or Irish or American churches may derive strength and inspiration to negotiate their own. The renewed ecclesiology which all this betokens is slowly pervading our Christian theology and practice.

Theological and Pastoral Conclusions

It would not be fair to suggest that in asking a moral theologian to study their situation and particularly the violence, the Rhodesian church people involved expected a series of categorical answers to precise questions. Part of the difficulty of such an assignment is that the questions keep changing, even in such an apparently defined aspect of the violence question as the justice of its goal or the definition of non-combatants. The Rhodesian church has to find its own answers and make its own responses. The first half of this book concentrated on how traditional and contemporary theology might be fed into that process of discovering answers and making responses. The second half attempted to take it a stage further by confronting the actual situation in Rhodesia, including its historical roots, with the theological analysis. Further and fine application of this kind has to be attempted by the Rhodesian church itself. This will involve the continuing interchange between actual situation and theological understanding which this book has attempted. The last words and the first actions must therefore be left to the local church. A sympathetic outsider who has laboured to share some insider understanding in an effort to assist a truly insider response, may be pardoned for appending his own last words. They can be no more than my own tentative personal conclusions on the moral and pastoral answers and responses to be made to the situation in Rhodesia. I stress the tentative and personal character; they can only be tentative because even as I write, in the midst of the London negotiations, the situation is changing, perhaps radically. They are narrowly personal in so far as they exceed my academic analysis of tradition and situation. They do not necessarily follow from it. Their limitations are not necessarily due to the earlier analysis but reflect one person's final application of that analysis to very particular questions. The value of such conclusions for the reader then rests not on their acceptability or validity but on seeing them as further illustrations of how such conclusions may be drawn and of the risk which drawing conclusions always involves. It is a risk which the writer felt he could not in honesty shirk. Hence the value of the conclusions for him. Despite inevitable misunderstandings they are best presented as stark unargued theses. The background of argument is provided by the book. Besides, such conclusions (involving as they do personal perceptions and equations) are irreducible to and cannot be finally articulated in clear-cut argument. And they are not, as I said, the only conclusions possible from the arguments already examined.

Personal Conclusions

1. The basic injustice and source of violence in Rhodesia was the development of a discriminating and exploiting state, which became more obvious with UDI in 1965.

2. If one accepts the criteria of a just war as applying to a just revolution, the conditions for a just revolution were fulfilled, as far as they are ever likely to be, by the early 1970s in Rhodesia.

3. The manner of pursuing the violent revolution and of responding to it frequently violated the criterion of using 'just means' by attacks on innocent civilians, use of torture etc.

4. The Salisbury Agreement of March 1978 did not achieve the goal of restructuring the society to the point of making the rebels' cause unjust.

5. For the sake of Rhodesia's future, substantial changes in political, social and economic structures are required.

6. If such substantial changes adopt a socialist form they are not thereby anti-Christian.

7. For the sake of the future of Zimbabwe and the rest of Southern Africa, the philosophy, strategy and tactics of non-violent political change should be urgently developed.

8. The churches should assume some responsibility for such development.

9. The churches, through the Commission for Justice and Peace and other institutions, should combine to promote the kingdom values in society as a whole.

10. The churches should similarly continue to monitor respect for human rights in the future Zimbabwe.

11. The experience of the churches in Rhodesia provides both a salutary lesson in their earlier compromises with the colonialist-racist regime and real encouragement in their eventual break with it and resistance to it.

12. The outlines of a new ecclesiology or understanding and structuring of church responsibility and mission may be discerned in the responses of the Catholic church in Rhodesia to the regime over the past few decades.

13. Such a new ecclesiology, in the sharing of responsibility and power and in the promotion of justice as constituent parts of mission, could change the hierarchical and clerical face of the Church far outside the borders of Rhodesia.

14. The experience of a local church such as the Rhodesian can and should become a source of fresh understanding and inspiration for other local churches in similar and even quite diverse circumstances.

15. Theology and Christian practice have to seek a much closer relationship if their mutual enrichment is to be truly effective.

Epilogue

Since this book was begun in November 1978 and particularly since it was completed in November 1979, dramatic and permanent changes have occurred in what is now irrevocably Zimbabwe. The Lancaster House Agreement of December 1979 involving the leaders of the Patriotic Front (Robert Mugabe and Joshua Nkomo) as well as the parties to the Internal Settlement (of March 1978) led to the ending of Rhodesia's illegal status, the temporary restoration of British rule, the ending of guerrilla war with the return of the guerrillas to their homeland and the holding of free elections under British direction and with international observers in February of 1980. The overwhelming victory of Robert Mugabe and his Zanu-PF party in these elections, his designation as Prime Minister by the British Governor, Lord Soames, and his inclusion in his government of Joshua Nkomo and other members of his party, together with two white representatives from the Rhodesian Front party, have set the scene for the formal and internationally recognised independence of Zimbabwe on 18 April 1980.

There is no doubt that Zimbabwe's past will begin to look different from that of Rhodesia in the aftermath of independence. It would be simply too cynical to claim that the winners or conquerors always write or rewrite history. Yet the standard histories of Rhodesia in English always began their serious accounts with the preliminaries to and arrival of Rhodes's Pioneer Column in 1890. The long centuries of African inhabitation were scarcely mentioned and then principally because of the Africans' contact with the first Portuguese explorers and missionaries of the sixteenth century or with the later British explorers and missionaries in the middle to late nineteenth century. More significant was the presupposition that civilisation arrived with the Europeans. All this played a very serious ideological role in forming and sustaining white consciousness of superiority and subsequent white intransigence leading to the bloody events of the last fifteen years. This white story left no room for any African story and as this book has indicated could only accommodate the basic Christian story by seriously distorting it.

How will the Christian story, in its basic biblical form and in its particular historical Rhodesian and Zimbabwean form, fare in the new context? No doubt the past will look very different and some of the colonial and conquest associations of the missionaries will make very embarrassing reading. Yet the recent attempts by the church leaders to check, change and finally confront the white supremacists and the Smith regime should fare well in the new historical perspective of independence.

However the past is understood, and that understanding is important to the future, facing the future itself will present enormous challenges to the new state and to the Christian leaders. The statesmanship, generosity and imagination displayed by Robert Mugabe so far gives reason for hope. His political philosophy, drawing as he says on Marxism, Christianity and the African tradition, has yet to be fully elaborated and, more importantly, tested in the difficult processes of government. It gives no more reason for fear to the Christian churches than do a dozen competing philosophies throughout Africa and the world at large. Indeed it may give a lot more reason for hope if Mugabe's initial moves are adequate indication. The churches will have to reconsider their roles. The ultimate and urgent relation between faith and social justice will involve Christian commitment to fairness in development and distribution of material resources and effective participation in decisions about these. The church in service of the Kingdom will seek ways to operate in society that will support the state in the daunting task of enabling a war-weary and exploited people to achieve a just peace by entering increasingly into the fruits of their earth, the many valuable developments of the contemporary world and the opportunity for personal growth and social participation which herald in some partial and ambiguous measure the values of Christ's Kingdom. It is to be hoped that the courage and vision which at times inspired the churches in the last couple of decades will not desert them now. It is in such hope that this book is dedicated to the Zimbabwean churches, particularly my own Catholic church.

Enda McDonagh
1 April 1980

Appendix

Impressions of a Visit April—May 1978

The decision that the author of the eventual report should spend some time in Rhodesia was amply justified in the event. At least without such an experience his awareness of the real questions and problems of the church and of that society would be very remote and detached from the situation. The insider feel and insight which is an essential part of understanding these questions was at least initiated and to some extent developed during the visit.

1. Purpose, Scope and Limitations

The purpose of the visit was to elicit the moral and theological questions of Church members, episcopal, clerical, religious and lay, African and European, in regard to the political situation and the war. This determined the structure and scope of my travels, contacts and conversations. The time available and the geography to be covered placed serious restrictions on my capacity to fulfil my purpose in any complete way. However the organisation, hospitality and cooperation provided right through the country under the sponsorship of the individual bishops made my task much easier and enabled me to achieve in terms of access and contact far more than I could reasonably have expected.

As I was concerned primarily with the Catholic church's problems, I had in the time available to confine myself to this church's members. This had great advantages for me as a visitor with this particular project. It meant that I got a concentrated exposure to the diverse views of the diverse members of this church and could more easily connect and assimilate these views without having to integrate views of members of other Christian churches or of politicians. In this way I could hope to understand the felt problems of the Catholic church more quickly and clearly. The disadvantage was that I was unable to compare Catholic reactions with other Christian reactions and that in areas as complex as politics and warfare I had very little chance to meet the men actually engaged in political and military activity. It might be possible to remedy some of this in a subsequent visit. At the time I believe the right procedure was adopted.

2. Assessment of Approach, Contacts and Conversations

My approach was basically through the local bishop or his vicar. Mgr Reckter very kindly arranged this with the assistance of the Justice and Peace Commission. I visited the dioceses for varying lengths of time. I discussed the issues with each bishop or vicar (with the exception of the Archbishop of Salisbury who unfortunately had to be in Europe while I was in his diocese). With the cooperation of the bishops or vicars I met and spoke with a wide range of priests, religious and laity, African and European.

My first impression of these conversations is of the remarkable willingness of the people to discuss openly with me such difficult and delicate issues. Instead of regarding me as an interfering and ignorant foreigner (as they might easily have done), they showed not the slightest resentment or reluctance. Indeed, some of them expressed gratitude to the church authorities who had provided them with someone (however limited) to listen to their views and at times help to clarify them. This willingness and freedom were naturally most in evidence with individuals or small and coherent groups. In larger and more diverse groups there were understandable difficulties and inhibitions. I was fortunate enough to avoid such situations most of the time.

The second characteristic of these conversations which impressed was their honesty. Naturally it is more difficult for an outsider to assess this quality. (As an Irishman one might feel that honesty in such situations might well be in inverse proportion to willingness.) The honesty was conveyed to me by the seriousness of the participants, their clear awareness that what they were saying was not necessarily acceptable to me (e.g. some sharp criticism of my fellow-whites by Africans or of my fellow-countrymen by other whites), the risks some of them admitted they were taking in talking to me in such a manner about such issues, the consistency they displayed in answering follow-up questions and usually their evident and deep involvement in the situation itself.

This impression of honesty was reinforced by the trouble many people took to ensure that I spoke to people of quite different viewpoints from their own. Despite their involvement with a particular point of view, the fairness displayed by these people in sometimes personally arranging for me to talk to people known to them to be of a quite different point of view was quite impressive.

This fairness also emerged in some discussions of particular issues where arguments for a different attitude and understanding would be recognised as having some validity. In a paradoxical way this fairness was most striking among certain European clergy who were, as a whole, and this is a subject for later discussion, deeply and sometimes bitterly divided over the problems which concerned me. It would be too much to say that all my contacts and conversations were characterised by willingness and honesty. Unfairness at times reflected their honesty.

In the discussions themselves, the degree of political awareness and the sophistication of analysis frequently surprised me. This applied particularly to the African laity, whose formal educational background was generally much more limited than that of their white counterparts, but whose ability for analysis and articulation was frequently superior. Many examples of this could be given in relation to the causes of the war, the responsibility for particular atrocities, the content of the Internal Settlement, the achievements of the interim government or the prospects of a communist Zimbabwe in the future. It was not that I necessarily agreed with the arguments or conclusions but they impressed as having been thought through on the basis of definite information and experience.

The most difficult assessment to make is how far my contacts and conversations gave a fair and representative account of the views and attitudes within the Rhodesian church. The numbers I encountered were necessarily small, proportionately of laity, and absolutely of Sisters and Brothers. The proportion of priests, African and European, was very high but not consistent throughout the dioceses. In one or two dioceses I met almost 100 per cent, in another over 50 per cent, but in others much fewer. The quality of the contact with priests also varied. In the areas where I met fewer, I had sometimes more opportunity for personal or small-group discussion. My deeper contact with African priests was limited to five or six.

The laity I encountered in three dioceses were mainly African but not disproportionately so. As they were collected rather haphazardly on the basis of contacts by bishops or priests they seemed to represent no particular lobby and in that sense were probably quite representative. The Africans were disproportionately from townships but usually turned out to have originated in the Tribal Trust Lands and to have regular contact with their families there.

If one were engaged in a serious sociological study, the size and make-up of my sample, at least among the African laity, would be totally inadequate. However as I was interested in discovering and discussing ideas and attitudes and types of argument within a narrow range of interest with a view to raising moral and theological questions, the limitations of the sample may be less important. Such ideas and attitudes and arguments covered a very wide range and offered a valid basis for my work as long as I do not attempt to quantify their support among the people or conclude that other ideas or attitudes do not exist or do not bear on my work. Quantification is not important to my project. The more basic ideas are likely to include in some fashion the more exotic variations which I did not experience. At any rate these are limitations within which every study of this kind has to be done.

3. Issues Discussed

Although my brief was relatively well-defined before I began my visit to Rhodesia, I did not feel that I should dictate the course of my various conversations or confine my inter-locutors to any pre-selected set of issues. So after explaining briefly my purpose and interest, I usually let the conversation take its own course, putting in the odd question or suggesting other aspects or viewpoints and usually adding questions at the end on matters overlooked or neglected. For obvious reasons I did not use a tape-recorder or, at the smaller meet-ings, take any notes. I made brief summaries each evening of what had occurred. All this led to a certain untidiness in the conversations themselves and a possibly distorting compres-sion and selectivity in the subsequent notes. Yet I believe that the account of issues presented here fairly represents the many conversations I had over three weeks. I may add that despite the amount of travel involved, I managed to fit in quite a remarkable number of conversations per day. A typical example of a travel day was conversing from 8.30 a.m. to 3.00 p.m. with African and European priests in the Wankie area, flying to Salisbury and having a long session with a group of white laity that evening. In these conversations diverse views on every issue were expressed. This diversity sometimes amounted to total mirror-image reversal. I will try to do justice to the diversity in reporting on each issue.

(a) The Historical and Political Background to the Present Situation

The majority viewpoint, with important reservations, saw the white-dominated structure of society with all its exploita-tion of and discrimination against the African population as the basic source of the political instability in the country and of the gradual escalation of the violence to its present propor-tions. This was the unanimous view of the Africans I talked to, lay, clerical and religious. It was, I believe, the majority view of the European clergy and religious but the minority view of the European laity. Among the European supporters of this view, some reservations were expressed in regard to the ignoring or minimising of what the Europeans had done for the Africans and for the development of the country.

This point was naturally more emphasised by the Europeans who saw the source of the conflict not in the internal structures and practices of Rhodesia but in external forces and their trained agitation and 'terrorists'. Some of these Europeans would grant the need for reform, social, economic, and political, but insisted this was on the way and could not be hurried beyond the stage of readiness of the African population. That the basic issue was one of political injustice amounting for many to institutional violence was accepted by the vast majority (Group I) but vigorously disputed by a minority, all whites, but both clerical and lay (Group II).

(b) The Violence and its Moral Evaluation

All the people I spoke to regretted the violence and deplored the atrocities, attributed in varying degrees to both sides. However, the two groups already distinguished tended to view the violence in relation to the previous political situation rather differently. Naturally, for the second group in section (a) but also for some people in the first group, the violence of the 'terrorists' (their word) could not be justified by the (alleged) discrimination and injustice against the Africans. In no sense then could they see this as a just war or revolution against the established order.

Among the first group, for whom the basic source of the problem was the discrimination and injustice, there was a variety of attitude in regard to the moral evaluation of the fighting by the guerrillas (their word) or the 'boys' (the African people's word). Deferring for the present any discussion of the 'Internal Settlement' which added to the confusion, I may illustrate the diversity of attitude by relating a brief catechesis which I devised in the course of three discussions. Here I consider only replies from Group I who saw the injustice as the basic problem.

Q. Given the serious injustice, and the progress of previous negotiations, do you consider the Africans' resort to violence was inevitable?

A. Almost unanimously, yes, from Group I.

Q. If inevitable do you consider it understandable?
A. Almost unanimously, yes.

Q. If understandable, do you consider it morally excusable?
A. Some hesitations but majority, yes.

Q. Do you therefore consider this a just war of liberation?
A. Much more hesitation, many noes and many yeses and many don't knows.

Q. If it is a just war for the Africans, then it must be an unjust war for the Security Forces, as it cannot be just on both sides. So you accept the Security Forces are involved in an unjust war?
A. Very few answered yes but some did and one man related refusing absolution to a member of the Security Forces on this basis.

The usefulness of this exercise and the responses to the questions must be carefully assessed. Its main value lay in the sorting out of ideas it demanded of people who, while trained in the classical moral theology of a just war, were unable in the actual situation, with all its tension and emotion, to use that theology. Against this must be put the unexpected nature of the questioning and the short time in which they had to reply. For these reasons more people adopted an 'I don't know' attitude as the questions progressed. Another influence was of course the nature of the war, particularly the atrocities against the civilian population and missionaries themselves, which the classical theology also took into account in assessing a just war. Related to this and deeply influential with all was the traditional, instinctive Christian oppostion to violence, which is not really compatible with the 'just war' theory. Alternatives to war had not seriously been discussed or developed in Rhodesia any more than they have amongst most Christians opposed to injustice around the world. Questions about the conduct of war and alternatives to it underline the limitations of the just war theory as an adequate Christian response to any situation. They require further more detailed treatment.

(c) Conduct of the War

All the people I spoke to expressed horror at the atrocities suffered by the civilian population, including white missionaries. Supporters of the justice of the cause did not condone in any way atrocities attributed to the guerrillas. Their attitudes, however, to the general conduct of the war, particularly the Africans' attitudes, differed significantly from the attitudes of those who conceded certain injustices but did not see them as at all sufficient to explain, excuse or justify the violence (Group II).

The sympathisers with the cause (Group I) entered three qualifications about the atrocities attributed to the guerrillas. Some of them at least were the work of the Selous Scouts of the Security Forces. Examples given were the killing of Bishop Schmitt and his companions and the killing of the Jesuits and Dominicans at the Musami mission. This attribution of atrocities against missionaries to the Security Forces was usually rejected by Group II both in the particular instances given and in general. The second qualification by Group I was that the atrocities committed by the Security Forces (Selous Scouts or others) were at least equal to those of the guerrillas. The forcible removal of people to particular villages and their treatment there, the terrorisation of villagers in the bush, the torture of suspects and shooting of curfew-breakers were instanced among others. For Group I this was all the more reprehensible in that it was being done in the name of 'law and order' and even in alleged defence of 'Christian civilisation and standards'. Group II conceded that certain atrocities and excesses were to be attributed to the Security Forces but some regarded some of these as at least understandable and even justifiable in view of the basic justice of their cause and their difficulties in protecting the people against the unjustified attacks of the 'terrorists'.

A third qualification of the condemnation of the excesses of the guerrillas mentioned by Group I was the inevitability of such events in any war and particularly in guerrilla warfare, due to inefficiency, indiscipline, lack of coordination, misinformation, fear and frustration. The absence of centralised control among the guerrillas in this field and of ultimate political control of the military wing were suggested. In this connection many people from Group I reported growing indiscipline among the guerrillas in certain areas and their recourse to drink, drugs and girls. Some Group II members appealed to this 'inevitability' as a further reason for ruling out war and violence as a means of liberation or reform. Hovering at the back of many of these arguments there seemed to be the difficulty about how far the church should and could denounce clear-cut injustices without taking some responsibility for the means to be adopted or actually adopted in removing them. It further reveals the church's problem about claiming to be a moral guide in social as in personal affairs and at the same time to be outside and above politics. There seemed some grain of truth in the cynical comment that when the church condemns the others it is exercising moral leadership, when it condemns us it is interfering in politics.

(d) Alternatives to Violence

Perhaps the most disappointing feature of the discussions was the lack of awareness or even interest in effective alternatives to violence in promoting radical social change. Many Africans pointed out the legal and practical difficulties of organising even the mildest of protests. This was confirmed during my stay by the treatment of university students who protested in apparently a very disciplined way against the Internal Settlement, and the contrasting treatment of the middle-class white women who threw eggs and fruit at the British Foreign Secretary's car. Allied to this practical argument was the whole history of demonstration, protest and negotiation over twenty years and the negative repressive responses of the government. Yet this course of events which was not dissimilar to the histories of India or the American South, does not entirely explain the lack of attention to the philosophy and techniques developed by Gandhi and Martin Luther King. The harshest critics of the violence could not suggest any effective alternatives along these lines either, contenting themselves with moral condemnations of the violence, appeals for peace and reliance on methods that in the past at any rate could give the Africans little cause for encouragement. The problem of awakening — or at least encouraging — the African people by strong and clear denunciations of the immorality of the system without taking sufficient thought for effective moral means of change is at least partly responsible for the confusion and division affecting certain sections of the church in Rhodesia. And while many may wearily think it is too late to think of such matters now, a view of the whole situation in Southern Africa of which Rhodesia is an integral part would, I believe, suggest otherwise. For example, whatever happens in the Republic of South Africa over the next 10—20 years will crucially affect Zimbabwe/Rhodesia. How far the inevitable changes there are achieved violently or non-violently will have repercussions north of the Limpopo which the church will have to confront. Will it still be sufficient to denounce injustice and outlaw violence? Or can Rhodesia provide support and encouragement for non-violent rather than violent leaders and freedom-fighters?

(e) Internal Settlement

To some this discussion of the war, its cause, its conduct and the alternatives might seem to have been already overtaken by the event of 3 March, the signing of the Agreement by one white and three black leaders to achieve an internal settlement leading to transfer of power from the white minority to the black majority. Although this agreement did introduce a whole new and, for many, confusing element and must be considered further, I do not think that the discussions reported are irrelevant or already outdated.

The war was and is still going on. It is basically the same war being fought by mainly the same people for what they believe to be mainly the same reason, the genuine liberation of the people of Zimbabwe and the genuine transfer of power. It is the belief not only of the guerrillas and their supporters but of many of their current opponents that the war directly or indirectly (through its economic effects) brought the Smith regime to the negotiating table and to the stage of the March Agreement. It would have been politically naïve to expect the guerrillas simply to surrender their arms before 31 December, the promised day of independence. In some of their attempts to achieve a cease-fire, agents of the Executive Council conceded that the guerrillas would hold their positions and their arms until Independence Day but should simply cease fighting. According to some sources they would in turn be left unmolested by the Security Forces. Given the necessary watchfulness of the Africans in view of previous settlement failures, it would not, it was argued, be unreasonable for them to maintain their military strength and presence even if the war should be de-escalated. And of course the very nature of the war with its slow build-up and the loose structure of the guerrilla forces would permit only gradual de-escalation. Apart then from taking sides on the merits of the Internal Settlement itself and the genuine commitment of the white regime to real transfer of power (something that could not be easily and quickly done by the Africans as a whole), the continuance of the war as a fact and for many an understandable fact justified, I believe, the discussions previously recorded.

Yet the Internal Settlement clearly made a difference to people's views of the war, if only to confirm them. For many Europeans this was the end of the affair. Whatever justification there might have been for guerrilla warfare and violence hitherto, that had been removed by the attainment, as they saw it, of the basic aims of the war, 'one man, one vote', majority African rule and the consequential removal of the various other injustices and discrimination. For those opposed to the violence in any event, the settlement provided the crowning answer. Many Europeans who found the violence understandable or even justifiable previously, believed that it was no longer so. Others were simply confused, appreciating the points outlined earlier about African difficulty in suddenly and simply stopping the war. One interesting feature of European reaction, which I encountered here, is worth recording. The tiny percentage of European laity who generally supported the aims of the guerrillas and accepted the fighting as inevitable, even justifiable, did not, unlike the clergy of similar views, regard the settlement as even the beginnings of a satisfactory solution and the war therefore as having lost any, moral justification it had in the past. Their views co-incided with the majority African viewpoint as I experienced it. In this discussion above, all the Africans displayed their capacity for sophisticated and even ingenious political analysis, however valid. Their opposition to the Settlement was almost unanimous and their reasoning at least coherent and generally well-informed and consistent. In their awareness of the contents of the Agreement, and of the previous and subsequent course of events, they seemed usually much better informed than their European counterparts.

Three clusters of objections were raised in various ways by the different Africans I met. The most important were perhaps to the contents of the agreement itself, embracing the odd electoral arrangements, the guarantees about, as they saw it, continuing white control of the judiciary and security forces, and the question of the land. Some of these objections were rather simply expressed and they were not all voiced by each group or individual. They were, however, unmistakably known as weaknesses in the settlement to the Africans.

The point made by defenders of the settlement that all these matters could be sorted out once the Africans took over did not prove fully convincing to them partly because what was written was written, including in their view a ten-year white veto on basic change, but perhaps more importantly because of the people involved.

The second cluster of objections concerned the parties to the agreement and the parties outside it. Focal to this was a basic distrust of the Prime Minister, Ian Smith. His right to be called Prime Minister within the terms of the agreement was questioned and the continuance of the title was taken to confirm the suspicion that the agreement was a sham. As far as the black participants were concerned, Chief Chirau was dismissed as a puppet of Smith, Bishop Muzorewa was regarded with great affection and admiration as a good man but thought to have been out-manoeuvred by Smith and to some extent by Sithole who was recognised as able but not greatly trusted. The non-participation by the Patriotic Front leaders was seen as sufficient to condemn the agreement by some but at least as a great weakness in the African side by all.

The third cluster of objections centred on the achievements or lack of achievements by the Executive Council since 3 March. The release of detainees and the unbanning of ZAPU and ZANU seemed insignificant while the main discriminatory laws and practices remained. The co-Minister of Justice, Byron Hove, was dismissed for voicing what so many Africans were thinking and believing. Reports were circulating of closed meetings giving reassurances to Europeans that nothing had changed. This frame of mind, which I found in varying degrees among so many Africans, was balanced in some degree, by a desire for an end to the war and uncertainty about alternatives to the settlement.

(f) Alternatives to Settlement

Despite a certain war-weariness many Africans expressed themselves resigned to the fact that the war must go on until a proper settlement was reached. What that proper settlement would be they were less sure. One alternative which I put to them, a Marxist or Communist Zimbabwe, they almost unanimously rejected and regarded as unattainable in the new Zimbabwe.

The reasons for this rejection were again clear and consistent, however valid they may or may not have been. The first reason given was the naturally religious character of the African people. I was uncertain what to make of this either as a statement of fact or as a defence against Communism. The second reason was more tangible. In comparison with other African countries coming to independence Rhodesia enjoyed in certain sectors a developed economy both industrially and agriculturally. No leader seeking to retain power would dismantle this in the name of ideology but would seek to build on it. A mixed economy with both public and private enterprise was the only way forward for Zimbabwe. Again I was surprised and impressed at the level of argument produced here.

The third argument rested on what they considered the generally higher level of education among the African population, certainly compared with Mozambique and Angola.

This would mean a greater ability to participate in the shaping of the future of their country and a greater resistance to any kind of enforced ideology coming from outside. Whoever becomes leader and whoever forms the government will have to listen to the people, I was told.

Their vague vision was of some kind of African socialism in a state which would be properly multi-racial. The Europeans should remain full citizens as a matter both of principle and of expediency. Many of them had belonged there for generations. And whenever they or their families came, their expertise in various areas of life was badly needed. Many of the Europeans I spoke to, even those long committed to a free Zimbabwe, were much less optimistic about the effective rejection of a Marxist regime. The attitudes, slogans and behaviour of the guerrillas in recent months and particularly in the ZAPU areas displayed a new and virulent anti-religious attitude according to many European missionaries in these areas. The declarations of Marxism by Mugabe were quoted together with the training and arming of guerrillas in Communist countries or under Communist direction. The presence of Cuban 'advisers' with ZAPU forces in Zambia (subsequently admitted by Nkomo) added to the same conviction. Undoubtedly some European priests were greatly influenced by the attacks on mission-stations and killing of missionaries in their strong interpretation of Communist influence and presence. But it would be naïve to deny its reality.

The responses of Africans and Europeans who refused to take the Communist scare so seriously or to regard a Communist regime as inevitable did not deny the reality of this influence and presence. Apart from the reasons for African rejection of a Communist prospect already outlined, these critics maintained that the guerrillas and their political and military leaders naturally took their arms and their training wherever they could get them. As they could not get them from the West they naturally turned to the East. However, such an expedient, so the argument goes, does not necessarily involve ideological acceptance of Communism or future client-status in relation to the Communist states. It is argued further that Nkomo is in no sense a Marxist ideologue, more an old-fashioned nationalist with capitalist inclinations. And despite Mugabe's recent statement, neither his previous history nor the character of his movement suggest any clear-cut ideological stance of the kind displayed by Frelimo in Mozambique prior to independence.

The run of the argument was both fascinating and inconclusive. What was perhaps missing was any recognition of the European and South American attempts at rapprochement between Marxism and Christianity with their possible implications for Zimbabwe or Southern Africa in general. This provided an interesting contrast with my very brief experience in South Africa where clear attention is being given by African priests and theologians to the European and Latin American developments. The Rhodesians I met did not really elaborate on their positive vision of Zimbabwe and in particular what Zimbabwean socialism might look like, beyond distinguishing it from the 'capitalist' system in Kenya on the one hand and the Communist system in Mozambique on the other. Some churchmen's reluctance to discuss this was undoubtedly a genuine feeling that that was the business of the politicians and not of the church. This illustrates once again the difficulty of denouncing one system as immoral without offering to put anything in its place and of perhaps finding the replacement equally objectionable later while one maintains that moral guidance (i.e. negative criticism) is the church's role and not political guidance (i.e. positive proposals?). It is in helping to sort out this problem that the projected report may be most needed.

(g) The Future Course of Events

What emerged in discussions under this heading has to some extent been already considered — reaction to the settlement, and the future character of Zimbabwe. So I will concentrate here on a rather narrow thread of discussion, namely the future of the war and the further prospect of violence. Most people agreed that the war was not going to stop immediately, whether the settlement worked or not, whether it proved finally acceptable to the majority of Africans or not.

If it proved acceptable then the character of the war would change radically. If an African government with express majority support were really in charge of the security forces, augmented as some people hoped by former guerrillas, then both the moral and the psychological character of the war would change to the point of making the defeat of the resisting guerrillas feasible in a reasonable time. That is the view or at any rate the hope of supporters of the settlement. It would also attract the 'wait and see' Africans and Europeans and by definition would be acceptable to the majority of the population. The moral and psychological change would not necessarily guarantee victory but it would clearly weaken support for guerrillas within the country and attract support for the government from without. There could still be a long hard battle and much suffering to be endured by the African population in the rural areas in particular.

A variation on this scenario would be majority acceptance by Independence Day and a black government now pursuing the war more or less successfully. In this scenario, however, the difficulties discussed in the Agreement by its critics begin to take effect if real economic power or effective control of the security forces etc. remains with the European minority. These failures would be exploited by the opponents of the regime. The war would find a new purpose, socio-economic rather than nationalist liberation. The people would begin to support the guerrilla forces again. At this stage the struggle becomes more ideological and the support of Communist countries more likely to be influential if the opponents of the government triumph. The possibility of outside intervention on both sides could not be ruled out and a very bloody war would ensue before victory could be claimed or would be conceded by either side. The clear lesson to be drawn is that not only must the Internal Settlement prove acceptable to the majority now to end the war but the radical changes demanded and expected by so many Africans must quickly follow.

A somewhat similar pattern may emerge if the Internal Settlement is not accepted — an escalation of the war with a stronger ideological bias and greater Communist involvement.

If the West has not been identified with the settlement and if the Patriotic Front wins, as it must if the settlement is not accepted, the ideological commitment and eastern influence may not be strong. However, the success of the Patriotic Front may not end the violence. A power-struggle between the two parties to the Front is not to be ruled out. And it could occur for personal, ideological or tribal reasons. Perhaps for all three, simultaneously or successively, leading to incalculable suffering for the people of Zimbabwe.

Even when that is all sorted out, the new Zimbabwe will become a vulnerable front-line state of a South Africa likely to be subject to increasing harassment and possible guerrilla warfare with its guerrillas and their sympathisers seeking training and refuge in friendly front-line states. Will Zimbabwe be able to distance itself from this struggle? If not, what problems will South African guerrillas and refugees pose for it? What are the prospects of retaliatory or 'hot pursuit' raids by South African security forces? What will be the church's attitude and role in all this?

This very structure and gloomy pattern may be preempted at different points along the line but the risks are undoubtedly there. A caring church must confront the risks, seek to promote the best and yet be prepared for the worst. But that is to move into the final section of the report of my impressions on the role and state of the church.

4. Role and State of the Church

What I have already reported of the welcome and cooperation which I received at all levels of church life as well as of the openness, honesty and fairness of the people I talked to, naturally aroused my admiration for the church in Rhodesia as it struggles with almost intractable problems. The courage and good spirits which so many church members displayed in the most difficult conditions must constitute a significant witness to the gospel they bear. And this gospel was incarnated in a care and concern for the people which was extraordinarily impressive. Given the personal resources I encountered in the Rhodesian church, one felt that it must come through this period of suffering and darkness strengthened and purified.

(a) The Church's Stance on Injustice

Even hurried reading of the Bishops' Statements over almost twenty years now reveals how seriously and courageously they have faced up to the injustices under which the Africans suffer. My African contacts were well aware of this and the few people from other churches that I met confirmed for me the key-role played by the RCBC and its Commission for Justice and Peace in giving eloquent witness to the truths of Christ in face of racial, economic and political exploitation and oppression. The difficulty involved in denouncing injustice and so encouraging movements for radical change without being able to provide alternatives to violence we have already seen. The difficulty is not one peculiar to the Rhodesian situation. The violence itself and particular atrocities by both sides came in for severe moral condemnation. Given the different attitudes to the injustice and the violence examined earlier, particularly among European Catholics, one inevitably found very different assessments of the value and fairness of those condemnations. While African Catholics were fairly unanimous in support of the church's criticism of atrocities by the security forces, particularly praising the work of the Commission for Justice and Peace in pursuing particular instances of torture and cruelty, European Catholics were divided. The lay European Catholics I met were usually critical and even hostile but there were several notable exceptions. The clergy were deeply divided on the church's stance in regard to the injustice and the violence and some were bitterly critical of individual bishops and of the Commission for Justice and Peace.

(b) Divisions in the Church

The most distressing feature of the church which I experienced during my visit was undoubtedly the divisions among the clergy over the whole issue of the church's attitude to injustice and violence. I found at times an animosity and mistrust that showed a frightening lack of understanding or even communication. I tried to structure this division for some of my priest contacts on a basis which seemed to be helpful to them in understanding their own position and that of others.

As I saw it, while the clergy could not be neatly divided into two or any number of groups, they did tend to cluster at two ends of a spectrum. At one end were the people for whom the social and political injustice, the institutional violence was primary. The war and the physical violence was secondary to that and derived from it. This did not mean that they automatically justified the war or, indeed, that they justified it at all. Some did not. And no one condoned the atrocities committed against the missionaries and the civilian population. Yet they were always looking beyond them to what they believed was the real source of the violence and so they appeared 'soft' on violence to the other group for whom the violence as endured by the people and the missionaries was primary. This violence was predominantly the work of the guerrillas, although they did not deny or condone excesses by the security forces. With this primary preoccupation with the violence went an acknowledgment of certain injustices and exploitation. However, because for them this was now secondary, they seemed to people in the other group to be playing down the injustices to the point of effectively ignoring them. As each group became more obsessed with its own pre-occupation there was a tendency to shout past one another, leading to enormous misunderstanding and mistrust.

In practice the mistrust was fostered by the very delicate and dangerous situations in which people lived. Missionaries tended to be caught between the guerrillas and the security forces. Depending on their primary preoccupation, the injustice or the violence, they tended to align themselves, perhaps unconsciously and out of need for protection for their people as well as themselves, with the guerrillas or the security forces. In many instances alignment would be much too strong a word, in others too weak. But given their man-in-the-middle situation they tended to trust a little more to one side or the other, to expect protection a little more easily from one side or the other. Of course without any such align-ment (even unconscious), or against whatever alignment they did have missionaries found themselves compelled for humanitarian reasons as well as for the protection of themselves and their people to cooperate with fighting units in terms of providing food, clothing, medicine and other assistance. Such cooperation with either side would not always be forced but might be given freely out of conviction. However, decisions and practices of this kind make them naturally wary of talking to other people and particularly to people whose primary preoccupation and possible alignment was known to be different from their own. In such an atmosphere mistrust festered and rumours flew.

It would be foolish to deny that psychological, cultural and geographical factors (urban area or bush, ZANU or ZAPU territory) must play a role in these polarisations. It would be equally foolish for an outsider — or perhaps anybody — to try to analyse the situation completely in terms of such factors with a view to curing it. Such analysis, which would be necessarily very crude, is more likely to intensify the polarisation and eliminate any possibility of communication which must be urgently re-established between different groupings in the Rhodesian church.

I had not sufficient time and opportunity to probe the divisiveness further, particularly as it affected African and European priests. My opinion, based on such limited experience as I had, would suggest that while the Africans were naturally watchful and wary in the presence of Europeans, the present violent situation had not led to any mistrust and bitterness in relation to European priests generally. The divisions I observed among the clergy were happily not on the racial lines, African v. European. I am still very conscious of the commitment of the European priests to the people, African and European, and of the daily sacrifices they make for them. I must also stress again the fairness which many of them displayed in ensuring that I would have an opportunity to hear the other point of view. Yet there can be no denying or ignoring the existence and depth of the division and the threat it poses for the work of the church.

(c) Church Leadership

The leadership which the church had given in two decades

on the injustice and exploitation could, I believe, set a head-line for the world. Despite the confusion and division on the relation of injustice and violence, that leadership retains its impact for Catholic and non-Catholic, African and European alike. But in the new situation emerging and partly expressed in the March agreement, new problems and difficulties are presenting themselves at a rate which could prove paralysing for church leadership. At least the social complexity of these new problems, no longer to be analysed in literal black and white terms and the theological and ,astoral understanding they require, will make enormous fresh demands on the church for thought-through, firm and sensitive leadership.

With the war continuing, some of the old problems remain on the relation between political reform and violence, the possible moral justification of such violence and the neces-sary moral limits to all violence. The question of Christian alternatives to violence will certainly remain on the agenda.

And with or without the war the shape of the new Zim-babwe must exercise the minds and wills of the church, but how can the church show leadership without being accused of interfering in politics or actually doing so? Can it give moral guidance in social and political affairs without giving some positive content and so being once again dragged into the political arena? Is its job over when it criticises the old injustice or at any rate when the transfer of power takes place? Does it concern the church how it takes place? Should it therefore have and have voiced a thought-out reaction to the Internal Settlement? Or should it, as even some African opponents of the settlement said to me, stay on the side-lines now and leave the matter to the Africans and their politicians?

Is its role a communal one as church acting at all levels and in coordinated fashion to shape the future society? Or is that work for individual politicians and citizens whom it educates and spiritually nourishes? Can such individual activity be regarded as work of the church properly and fully? Is that the only way open to the church to promote the kingdom in society?

And what of its role when the new Zimbabwe is established? Will it be as outspoken in its denunciation of injustice and in calling for radical change where that is needed? Can it afford to be if, while the political leadership is African and local, the church leadership is primarily European and expatriate? What will be the role of a Commission for Justice and Peace in such a state? Who will lead and staff it?

How will the church evaluate and react to possible new ideologies and structures? Will there be a simplistic rejection of Marxist society should the danger threaten and a shallow accommodation with Marxist power should that threat succeed? If the Marxist threat proves a myth what alternative society will the church promote and how? Will it adjust equally easily in turn to some version of African socialism or yet another version of African capitalism, in either instance becoming marginalised itself in a materialist, consumer-orientated society? What are its responsibilities to traditonal African values? How can it discharge them?

It would be possible to go on listing more or less important tasks which the church leadership will in one form or another have to face. Two main groups are already evident: transfer of power within the church itself and the shaping of the new Zimbabwe. One is an ecclesial and the other a moral-political task. Both are clearly bound up with another task, that of the Christian prayer and spiritual being of the Catholics of Zimbabwe. To develop a prayer and spirituality that are relevant to the people and structures of the church and wider society, and that will transform them, is perhaps the greatest challenge facing the church leadership today. But it should be prayer and spirituality relevant to and transforming of people and structures. Any other kind is an evasion of reality, particularly the ultimate reality of God.

Bibliography

I. Church and Politics

Alfaro, Juan, *Christian Hope and the Liberation of Man*, Rome/Sydney: F. J. Dwyer 1978.

Anderson, Gerald H. and Stransky, Thomas F., CSP (ed.), *Mission Trends No. 4: Liberation Theologies*, New York/Toronto: Paulist Press. Grand Rapids, Mich.: Wm. B. Eerdmans 1979.

Amstutz, Josef, et al. (ed.), *Kirche und Dritte Welt im Jahr 2000*, Zurich, Einsiedeln, Cologne: Benziger 1974.

Arthur, John and Shaw, William H. (ed.), *Justice and Economic Distribution*, Englewood Cliffs, NJ: Prentice-Hall 1978.

Bauer, Fr Gerard (ed.), *Towards a Theology of Development; an Annotated Bibliograhy*, Geneva: Sodepax 1970.

Baur, Jörg, (ed.), *Zum Thema Menschenrechte; Theologische versuche und Entwürfe*, Stuttgart: Calwer 1977.

Bennett, John C., *The Radical Imperative*, Philadelphia, Penn.: Westminster Press 1975.

Bigo, Pierre, SJ, *The Church and Third World Revolution*, trans. Sr Jeanne Marie Lyons, Maryknoll, NY: Orbis 1977.

Bonino, José Miguez, *Christians and Marxists*, Grand Rapids, Mich: Wm. B. Eerdmans, 1976.

Bonino, José Miguez, *Revolutionary Theology Comes of Age*, London: SPCK/Philadelphia: Fortress Press, 1975.

Bright, John, *The Kingdom of God*, Nashville: Abingdon, 1953.

Bühlmann, Walbert, *The Coming of the Third Church*, Maryknoll, NY: Orbis 1977.

Chenu, Marie-Dominique, La *'doctrine sociale' de l'Eglise comme idéologie,* Paris: Cerf 1979.

Desmond, Cosmas, *Christians or Capitalist? Christianity and Politics in South Africa,* London: Bowerdean Press 1978.

Dummett, Michael, *Catholicism and the World Order,* London: CIIR 1979.

Eagleson, John (ed.), *Christians and Socialism,* trans. John Drury, Maryknoll, NY: Orbis 1975.

Fierro, Alfredo, *The Militant Gospel,* London: SCM 1977.

Gager, John G., *Kingdom and Community,* Englewood Cliffs, NJ: Prentice-Hall 1975.

Garaudy, Roger, *From Anathema to Dialogue: A Marxist Challenge to the Christian Churches,* New York: Herder and Herder 1966.

Geffre, Claude and Gutierrez, Gustavo, *The Mystical and Political Dimension of the Christian Faith,* New York: Herder and Herder 1974.

Girardi, Giulio, *Marxism and Christianity,* Dublin/Sydney: Gill 1968.

Gremillion, Joseph, *The Gospel of Peace and Justice; Catholic Social Teaching since Pope John,* Maryknoll, NY: Orbis 1976.

Grenholm, Carl-Henric, *Christian Social Ethics in a Revolutionary Age,* Uppsala: Verbum 1973.

Gutierrez, Gustavo, *A Theology of Liberation,* trans/ed. Sr Caridad Inda and John Eagleson, Maryknoll, NY: Orbis 1973.

Haughey, John C. (ed.), *The Faith that does Justice,* New York/Toronto: Paulist Press, 1977.

Hebblethwaite, Peter, *The Christian-Marxist Dialogue and Beyond,* London: Darton, Longman & Todd 1977.

Hengel, Martin, *Property and Riches in the Early Church,* London: SCM 1974.

Hengel, Martin, *Christ and Power,* trans. Everett R. Kalin, Philadelphia: Fortress Press 1977.

Hessel, Dieter T., *Beyond Survival: Bread and Justice in Christian Perspective,* New York: Friendship Press 1977.

Irish Bishops' Pastoral, *The Work of Justice,* Dublin: Veritas 1977.

John Paul II, Pope, *Redemptor Hominis,* Washington D.C.: United States Catholic Conference 1979.

Lane, Dermot A. (ed.), *Liberation Theology; An Irish Dialogue.* Dublin: Gill and Macmillan 1977.

Lehmann, Karl, *Theologie der Befreiung.* Einsiedeln: Johannes 1977.

Machoveč, Milan, *A Marxist Looks at Jesus,* London: Darton, Longman & Todd 1976.

Maritain, Jacques, *True Humanism,* New York: Charles Scribner's Sons 1938.

Maritain, Jacques, *Man and the State,* Chicago: University of Chicago Press 1951.

McDonagh, Enda, *Doing the Truth,* Dublin: Gill and Macmillan/Notre Dame, Ind.: University of Notre Dame Press 1979.

McDonagh, Enda, *Social Ethics and the Christian,* Manchester: Manchester University Press 1979.

Metz, Johann Baptist, *Theology of the World,* trans. William Glen-Doepel, New York: Seabury Press 1969.

Metz, Johann Baptist, *Glaube in Geschichte und Gesellschaft,* Mainz: Matthias-Grünewald 1977.

Metz, J. B. and Jossua, Jean-Pierre (ed.), *Christianity and Socialism,* New York: Seabury Press 1977.

Miller, Allen O. (ed.), *A Christian Declaration on Human Rights,* Grand Rapids, Mich.: Wm. B. Eerdmans 1977.

Miranda, José, *Marx and the Bible,* trans. John Eagleson, Maryknoll, NY: Orbis 1974.

Moore, Basil, *Black Theology: the South African Voice,* London: C. Hurst 1973.

Mouw, Richard J., *Politics and the Biblical Drama,* Grand Rapids, Mich: Wm. B. Eerdmans 1976.

Niebuhr, Reinhold, *Moral Man and Immoral Society,* New York: Charles Scribner's Sons 1932.

Niebuhr, H. Richard, *The Kingdom of God in America,* New York/London: Harper & Row 1937.

Norman, E. R., *Christianity and World Order,* London 1979.

Nyerere, Julius K. *Uhura Na Ujaama/Freedom and Socialism,* Oxford/New York: Oxford University Press 1968.

Pannenberg, Wolfhart, *Theology and the Kingdom of God*, Philadelphia: Westminster Press 1969.

Perrin, Norman, *Jesus and the Language of the Kingdom*, London: SCM Press 1976.

Schrey, Heinz-Horst, *et al.*, *The Biblical Doctrine of Justice and Law*, London: SCM 1955.

Schnackenburg, Rudolf, *God's Rule and Kingdom*, Freiburg: Herder 1963.

Sobrino, Jon, SJ, *Christology at the Crossroads*, London: SCM Press, 1978.

Soelle, Dorothee, *Suffering*, Philadelphia: Fortress Press 1975.

Sölle, Dorothee, *Politische Theologie*, Stuttgart/Berlin: Kreuz 1971.

Topel, L. John, SJ, *The Way to Peace*, Maryknoll, NY: Orbis 1978.

Torres, Sergio and Fabella, Virginia (ed.), *The Emergent Gospel*, Maryknoll, NY: Orbis 1978.

Volkomener, Helen, SP (ed.) *CELAM III Third Conference of the Latin American Bishops*, 1979.

Wicker, Brian, *First the Political Kingdom*, Notre Dame Ind.: University of Notre Dame Press 1967.

Wogaman, J. Philip, *Christians and the Great Economic Debate*, London: SCM 1977.

Yoder, John Howard, *The Christian Witness to the State*, Newton, Kansas: Faith and Life 1964.

Yoder, John Howard, *The Original Revolution*, Scottdale, Penn.: Kitchener/Ontario: Herald Press 1971.

Yoder, John Howard, *The Politics of Jesus*, Grand Rapids, Mich.: Wm. B. Eerdmans 1972.

II. Violence and Christian Faith

Ardrey, Robert, *The Territorial Imperative*, New York: Atheneum 1966.

Bainton, R. H., *Christian Attitudes Toward War and Peace*, New York: Abingdon 1960/London: Hodder 1961.

Bohannan, Paul (ed.), *Law and Warfare*, Austin/London: University of Texas Press 1967.

Bondurant, Joan V., *Conquests of Violence*, Los Angeles/London: University of California Press 1971.

Fanon, Frantz, *The Wretched of the Earth,* Middlex: Penguin 1967.

Fischer, Louis (ed.), *The Essential Gandhi,* New York: Vintage 1962.

Gandhi, M. K., *Non-Violent Resistance,* New York: Schocken 1961.

Gregg, Richard B., *The Power of Nonviolence,* New York: Schocken 1966.

Holmen, Arthur F., *War and Christian Ethics,* Grand Rapids, Mich: Baker Book House 1975.

Honderick, Ted, *Political Violence,* Ithaca, NY: Cornell University Press 1976.

Irish Council of Churches, *Violence in Ireland,* Dublin: Veritas and Belfast: Christian Journals 1976.

Marrin, Albert (ed.), *War and the Christian Conscience: From Augustine to Martin Luther King, Jr.,* Chicago: Henry Regney 1971.

McDonagh, Enda, *Gift and Call,* Dublin: Gill and Macmillan 1975.

Potter, Ralph B., *War and Moral Discourse,* Richmond, Virginia: John Knox 1973.

Storr, Anthony, *Human Destructiveness,* New York: Basic Books 1972.

Walzer, Michael, *Just and Unjust Wars,* New York: Basic Books 1977.

West, Charles C., *Ethics, Violence and Revolution,* New York: Council on Religion and International Affairs 1969.

Wiener, Philip P. and Fisher, John (ed.), *Violence and Aggression in History of Ideas,* New Brunswick, NJ: Rutgers University Press 1974.

Woodcock, George, *Gandhi,* London: Fontana, Collins 1972.

III. The Rhodesian Context

Blake, Robert, *A History of Rhodesia,* London: Eyre Methuen 1977.

Bratton, Michael, *Beyond Community Development,* London: Catholic Insitute for International Relations (CIIR), 1978.

Carter, Gwendolen M. and O'Meara, Patrick (ed.), *Southern Africa in Crisis,* Bloomington/London: Indiana University Press 1977.

Cary, Robert and Mitchell, Diana, *African Nationalist Leaders in Rhodesian Who's Who,* Johannesburg: Africana Book Society, 1977.

Catholic Commission for Justice and Peace in Rhodesia (CCJP), *Civil War in Rhodesia,* London: CIIR 1976.

CCJP/CIIR, *The Man in the Middle,* London 1975.

CCJP/CIIR, *Rhodesia, the Propaganda War,* London 1977.

CCJP, *An Analysis of the Salisbury Agreement,* Salisbury 1978.

CIIR, *Rhodesia after the Internal Settlement,* London: CIIR/ Salisbury: CCJP 1978.

Clarke, Duncan G., *The Unemployment Crisis,* London: CIIR 1978.

Gann, L. H., *A History of Southern Rhodesia; Early Days to 1934,* London: Chatto and Windus 1965.

Gjerstad, Ole (ed.), *The Organizer; story of Temba Moyo,* Richmond BC, Canada: LSM Press 1974.

Gilmurray, John, *et al., The Struggle for Health,* London: CIIR, 1979.

Glasswell, M. E. and Fashole-Luke, E. W. (ed.), *New Testament Christianity for Africa and the World,* London: SPCK 1974.

International Defence and Aid Fund (IDAF), *Zimbabwe: The Facts about Rhodesia,* London 1977.

IDAF, *Rhodesia: Why Minority Rule Survives,* London 1979.

IDAF, *Ian Smith's Hostages, Political Prisoners in Rhodesia,* London 1976.

International Labor Office (ILO), *Labour Conditions and discrimination in Southern Rhodesia (Zimbabwe),* Geneva: ILO 1978.

Kapungu, Leonard T., *Rhodesia: The Struggle For Freedom,* Maryknoll, NY: Orbis 1974.

Kay, George, *Rhodesia: A Human Geography,* New York: Africana 1970.

Lamont, Bishop Donal, *Speech from the Dock,* Essex: Kevin Mayhew, 1977.

Leys, Colin, *European Politics in Southern Rhodesia,* Oxford: Clarendon Press 1959.

Linden, I., *In Responsible Hands, Church and State in the Making of Zimbabwe-Rhodesia,* London: Longmans 1980.

Mason, Philip, *The Birth of A Dilemma,* Oxford/New York/ Toronto: Oxford University Press 1958.

Mlambo, Eshmael, *Rhodesia: the Struggle for a Birthright,* London: C. Hurst 1972.

Mozambique-Zimbabwe: One Struggle, London: Mozambique Solidarity Action, 1977.

Niemann, Rolf, *Von Rhodesien zu Zimbabwe,* Frankfurt: Haag and Herchen 1976.

O'Callaghan, Marion, *Southern Rhodesia: the Effects of a Conquest Society on Education, Culture and Information,* UNESCO 1977.

Palley, Claire, *Zimbabwe-Rhodesia: Should the Present Government be Recognised?* London: CIIR 1979.

Partridge, Nan, *Not Alone: A Story for the Future of Rhodesia,* London: SCM 1972.

Plangger, Albert (ed.), *Rhodesia — the Moral Issue,* Gwelo: Mambo 1968.

Randolph, R. H., SJ, *Aspects of Catholic Life in Rhodesia,* Gwelo: Mambo 1974.

Randolph, R. H., SJ, *Church and State in Rhodesia 1969– 1971,* Gwelo: Mambo 1971.

Ranger, Terence O., *African Voice in Southern Rhodesia 1898–1930,* London: Heinemann 1970.

Ranger, Terence O. Weller, John (ed.), *Themes in the Christian History of Central Africa,* Los Angeles: University of California Press, 1975.

Rhodesian Catholic Bishops Conference (RCBC), *The Road to Peace,* Gwelo: Mambo 1976.

RCBC, *United . . . by Consent,* Gwelo: Mambo 1978.

Samkange, Stanlake, *Origins of Rhodesia,* London: Heinemann Educational 1969.

Sithole, Ndabaningi, *Obed Mutezo,* Nairobi: Oxford University Press 1970.

Synge, Richard (ed.), *New African Yearbook 1979,* London: IC Magazine 1979.

Vambe, Lawrence, *An Ill-fated People,* London: Heinemann 1972.

Vambe, Lawrence, *From Rhodesia to Zimbabwe,* Pittsburgh: Heinemann 1976.

Notes

Chapter One, pp. 15—28

1. For a more developed treatment of the ecumenical convergence on these issues cf. E. McDonagh, *Social Ethics and the Christian,* Manchester University Press 1979.

2. G. von Rad writes: 'there is absolutely no concept in the Old Testament with so central a significance for all relationships of human life as that of S^{e}dáqáh (justice/righteousness).' (*Old Testament Theology,* I, p. 370). H. H. Schrey in a study prepared for the World Council of Churches states: 'It can be said without exaggeration that the Bible, taken as a whole, has one theme: The history of the revelation of God's righteousness,' (*The Biblical Doctrine of Justice and Love,* p. 50) quoted from John R. Donahue, 'Biblical Perspectives on Justice' in John C. Haughey (ed.), *The Faith that does Justice,* New York 1977, p. 68.

3. cf. Pope John Paul II, *Redemptor Hominis,* par. 8—14.

4. cf. C.-H. Grenholm, *Christian Social Ethics in a Revolutionary Age,* Uppsala 1973, p. 105 ff.

5. For fuller development of this, cf. E. McDonagh, *Gift and Call,* Dublin 1975.

6. A phrase beloved of John Courtney Murray in his approach to these problems.

Chapter Two, pp. 29—55

1. A similar distinction was effectively developed by Jacques Maritain particularly in his work *Man and the State,* Chicago 1951. There are clear interconnections between

174

Murray and Maritain and both were significant in the development of Catholic teaching into Vatican II teaching on religious liberty.

2. cf. R. Schnackenburg, *God's Rule and Kingdom*, New York–London 1963; N. Perrin, *The Kingdom of God in the Teaching of Jesus*, London–Philadelphia 1976; W. Pannenberg, *Theology and the Kingdom of God*, Philadelphia 1969.

3. The 'high' theology of human rights which the Catholic Church now enjoys is evident in the speech of Pope John Paul II to the United Nations, 2 October 1979. In this he is echoing many predecessors, particularly Pius XII, John XXIII and Paul VI.

4. The literature on liberation theology is by now immense. The classical exposition is still probably G. Gutierrez, *A Theology of Liberation*, New York 1973; cf. D. Lane, (ed.), *Liberation Theology: An Irish Dialogue*, Dublin–New York 1977.

5. Again the literature is very extensive. For a historical account of recent developments cf. P. Hebblethwaite, *The Christian-Marxist Dialogue and Beyond*, London 1977. Useful analyses of the dialogue are J. M. Bonino, *Christians and Marxists*, London 1976, from within the Latin American perspective, and G. Girardi, *Marxism and Christianity*, Dublin 1968, from within a European perspective.

6. Julius K. Nyerere, *Uhuru Na Ujaama, Freedom and Socialism*, London 1968; cf. C. Desmond, *Christians or Capitalist? Christianity and Politics in South Africa*, London 1978.

Chapter Three, pp. 56–78

1. I have already dealt quite extensively with these problems in 'Human Violence: A Question of Ethics or Salvation' in *Gift and Call*, Dublin–New York 1975, pp. 138-66 and 'Violence and Political Change' in *Doing the Truth*, Dublin–Notre Dame 1979, pp. 138-52. A select bibliography will be given at the end of the book. References here will be kept to a minimum.

2. cf. Arthur F. Holmes, (ed.), *War and Christian Ethics,* Grand Rapids 1975 and A. Marrin, *War and The Christian Conscience: From Augustine to Martin Luther King Jr,* Chicago 1971.
3. Bishop A. F. Winnington-Ingram, speaking on 28 Nov. 1918, cited in Keith Bryant and Lyall Wilkes, *Would I Fight,* Oxford 1935, p. 43.
4. cf. Marrin, op.cit. p. 92.

Chapter Four, pp. 79–87
1. A more developed presentation of the ideas given here can be found in E. McDonagh, 'Prayer and Politics', *The Furrow,* September 1979; cf. C. Geffre and G. Gutierrez, (ed.), 'The Mystical and Political Dimension of Christian Faith', *Concilium* New Series 6/10, New York 1979; and J. Sobrino, *Christology at the Crossroads,* London–New York 1978.

Chapter Five, pp. 91–102
1. I am deeply indebted to Ian Linden for his history of the church in Rhodesia, *Church and State in Rhodesia 1959– 1979,* Mainz 1979. General historical works on Rhodesia are listed in the bibliography. More closely related to my own work is R. Niemann, *Von Rhodesian Zu Zimbabwe, Emanzipation der Afrikaner durch Guerillakampf oder Verfassungskonferenz,* Frankfurt 1976.
2. cf. Linden, op. cit. p. 31.
3. cf. A. Plangger, (ed.), *Rhodesia, the moral issue: Pastoral Letters of the Catholic Bishops,* Gwelo 1968, pp. 14–52.
4. cf. R. H. Randolph, *Church and State in Rhodesia, 1969– 1971: A Catholic View,* Gwelo 1971.

Chapter Six, pp. 103–12
1. cf. Linden, op.cit.; Niemann, op.cit.; T. Ranger, *Revolt in Southern Rhodesia 1896–7, A Study in African Resistance,* London 1967; S. Samkange, *Origins of Rhodesia,* London 1969; L. Vambe, *An Ill-fated People,* London 1972; id., *From Rhodesia to Zimbabwe,* London 1976.

Chapter Seven, pp. 113—34

1. Hansard, vol. 90, no. 21, 31 July 1975, cols. 1706, 1724 quoted in *Civil War in Rhodesia, A Report from the Rhodesian Catholic Commission for Justice and Peace*, London 1976, p. 33.
2. Linden, op.cit.